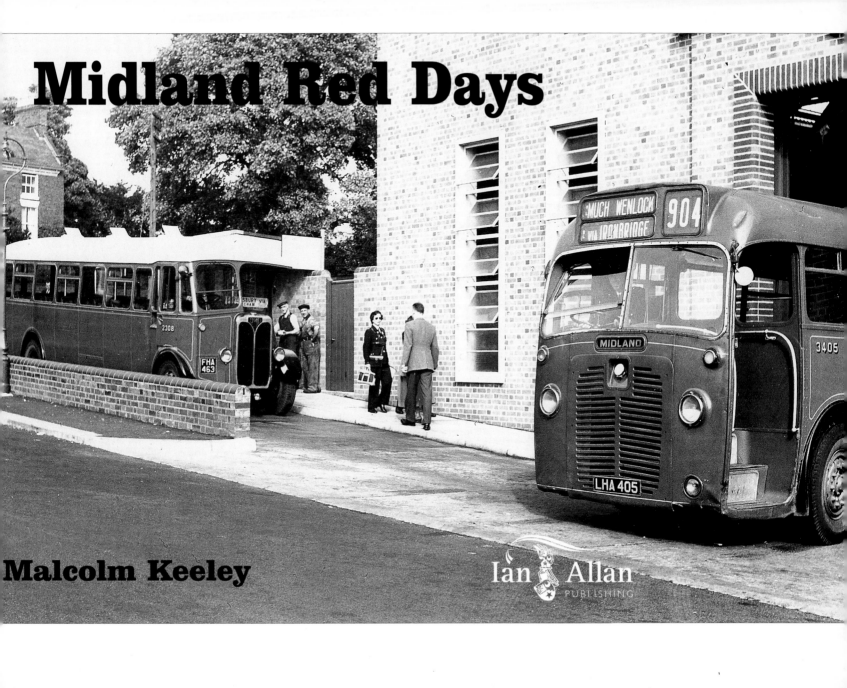

Midland Red Days

Malcolm Keeley

Title page: An animated early-1950s scene outside Midland Red's Wellington garage, with office, platform and craft staff all represented. The two buses show the design gap between Mr Shire's SOS vehicles and Mr Sinclair's BMMO buses. At some time 1949 S9 3405 has had a close encounter with a hedgerow along the narrow lanes, while 1939 SON 2308, with rebuilt body, prepares for a journey to Shrewsbury. The bodies on both buses were built by Brush to Midland Red design. *The Omnibus Society*

This page: The sunshine has brought duplicates to service 144 and FEDD 1584 stands in Hinckley Street, Birmingham, ready for a working as far as Worcester. This is one of the first production batch of 50 FEDDs, built in 1934 with bodies by Short Bros. Generally their bodies were not rebuilt, nor were their petrol engines replaced by diesels. Most were withdrawn between 1948 and 1950, but 1584 was one of a few refurbished in rather severe fashion by Samlesbury in 1948. Upon its withdrawal in 1952, the body was transferred to later FEDD 1822, which ran until 1956. *G. H. Stone*

Contents

First published 2001

ISBN 0 7110 2805 2

All rights reserved. No part of this book may be reproduced or transmitted in any form or by any means, electronic or mechanical, including photocopying, recording or by any information storage and retrieval system, without permission from the Publisher in writing.

© Malcolm Keeley 2001

Published by Ian Allan Publishing

an imprint of Ian Allan Publishing Ltd, Hersham, Surrey KT12 4RG. Printed by Ian Allan Printing Ltd, Hersham, Surrey KT12 4RG.

Code: 0108/B2

Introduction

It all began when somebody wandered into school in 1959 with the new Ian Allan *ABC Birmingham City Transport*. This was a revelation. We didn't know such publications existed; indeed, the previous edition was a decade earlier — just after we were born. For years I'd been working out by observation where bus deliveries started and finished — here it was all laid out, including why the Daimlers made different sounds — there were four different types of engine in them.

The next discovery was *ABC Midland Red*. This was on its fifth edition, yet knowledge of the series had eluded us. What a treasure trove of information it was, with a history, current fleet, Midland Red's own superb map and a list of garages. That fifth edition became the hardest-worked possession I ever had — it literally wore out.

The list of garages was irresistible. My knowledge of the Midlands leapt forward as we crawled over the map to discover exotic locations such as Ludlow or Malvern. Finding two Hartshills didn't help, but pooled knowledge confirmed the one with the bus garage was in Brierley Hill. (Actually the correct spelling is Harts Hill, before anyone writes in!).

Left: Whieldon's Green Bus of Rugeley typified the fascinating independent operators to be discovered as one travelled around by Midland Red. Interestingly this newly-acquired secondhand Guy No 20, seen in Rugeley in November 1959, has a link with the bigger company. Mr Sinclair had been Assistant Chief Engineer of Northern General Transport prior to his Midland Red appointment. NGT had radical ideas on vehicle design, introducing many side-engined buses during the 1933-8 period. NGT also persuaded AEC to produce more orthodox single-deckers with short cabs and compact engines and bonnets (in similar fashion to the Midland Red SON class) to maximise the area available for passengers. This individualism to an extent survived World War 2 and the loss of Mr Sinclair to Midland Red. Guy took over the mantle of providing NGT with compact-bonneted single-deckers, and in 1959/60 six of these 1949 Gardner 5LW-powered buses joined Green Bus. The 38-seat bodies were built by Brush. *Richard Butler*

But how to get to these places? Once again the bush telegraph worked — there was something called the 'Day Anywhere' ticket — 10s (50p) for adults and five bob for us. These had been available between the two wars, but had only been re-introduced in May 1958. Midland Red was then perceived as being expensive, but these tickets definitely had potential. One of us came across a Midland Red pamphlet of suggested 'Days Anywhere' from Birmingham, giving bus times and showing the normal fares to demonstrate the savings with the tickets. This provided the basis of our first excursions, but it was soon obvious that young lads with plenty of energy and a mission to see every Midland Red bus that existed could cover a lot more ground in a day.

The travel business in those days was in its infancy. A local chemist had a room at the back which offered travel tickets. These included 'Day Anywhere' tickets and, to assist enquiries, there was a full set of Midland Red's area timetables, which we were allowed to study. Wow! There was no stopping us now. Each school holiday would see us plotting marathon bashes by Midland Red. Looking back, it is astonishing that the staff tolerated these young lads cluttering up their small enclave for hours on end, bickering over the best route between, say, Stafford and Shrewsbury — all for a couple of child-value 'Day Anywhere' ticket sales.

Birmingham City Transport was, of course, our Number One interest and, living in Hall Green, we were also familiar with the lovely Leylands run by Stratford Blue on the joint 150 Birmingham–Stratford service. West Bromwich Corporation buses also worked into Brum, terminating alongside Snow Hill station. Odd contract buses were about, including Utilities with Black & White of Harvington and RTs with Jackson's of Castle Bromwich. With family holidays few and far between, buses in the world outside were a mystery. The 'Days Anywhere' began my long education in buses, and the industries that built and operated them.

Some places were difficult to reach from Birmingham, notably Hereford and Banbury. We began to discover alien buses, with an early lesson in exotica at Hereford, where we found Red & White vehicles, including Albions, plus a variety of independents on country routes. Receipt of the sixth edition of *ABC Midland Red* revealed that Leicester must be an early priority, because secondhand buses from acquired companies had entered the fleet there. These included Sentinels, although we had no idea then that these were any rarer than, say, Bristols.

My friend Stephen began to buy *Buses Illustrated* in 1960; this

was a bold move because his pocket money now had to fund the equivalent cost of an *ABC* every month! It was taken for granted that Midland Red would regularly produce something amazing like the first purpose-built motorway coaches or an underfloor-engined double-decker. But another fleet rivalled it for column space. This was Barton Transport, based in Nottingham. Barton's curved-screen AEC Regent Vs looked the last word in modernity. Then there was its low, low Loline, and countless secondhand purchases replacing earlier secondhand and strangely rebuilt buses. This called for a trip on the X99 Birmingham–Nottingham service, and the destination proved astonishing for buses with many different and contrasting fleets, whilst Barton was quite simply incomparable. I was now hooked on buses. My thirst for knowledge spread like a ripple caused by a pebble dropped in water, and I suppose, in due course, led to this book.

As mentioned earlier, families like mine were lucky if we had an annual holiday. Grandad took us regularly to the Cotswolds in his Ford car, but Dad didn't even take us out on the bus, so our adventures through Midland Red territory were an important voyage of discovery through industrial destruction, peaceful county towns and a variety of dramatic or featureless scenery. Our trips were never intended to be educational but, amidst the preoccupation with buses, an understanding of our surroundings had to seep in. Considering where we got to, I'm surprised how little our parents apparently worried about us. But this was 40 years ago. I don't recall any breakdowns or cancellations — buses were cruder but simpler, and Midland Red was only just tottering on the edge of the dark abyss of desperate staff shortages and falling revenue that would eventually destroy the company. Children (or 'kids', as they are nowadays inevitably known) today mature earlier, but many parents, I'm sure, would not turn them loose for fear of their being mugged, drugged or kidnapped. The nearest we got to an 'incident' was in deepest Herefordshire, when the conductor got himself into a lather about the antics of a pair of rustics of advanced years, chortling bucolically down the back of the bus. 'If you'm damaging moy bus, Barney Hayrick, I know where to come.' They'd probably been at the homebrew but, in its remoteness, that part of the world could be a little odd; reputedly one of the smaller towns has so much inbreeding that it's twinned with itself.

Our Midland Red was an undertaking that looked all of a piece. Okay, the surviving prewar buses designed under the lash of Mr Wyndham Shire looked quite different from the modernistic motors built under the equally brilliant D. M. Sinclair. But the D7 was clearly descended from the D1, and you could see the evolution of

Left: The independent operators' classic rural bus was the Bedford — cheap, economical and indefatigable — particularly the early-postwar OB model. Gatherings of them would be found in towns on market days, having brought in country-dwellers. This July 1959 line-up in Derby features LRB 158 (G. E. Taylor, Crich), ORE 359 (R. H. Steeples, Parwich), LRA 310 and JRB 953 (E. & H. Webster, Hognaston), EUN 318 (E. Carter, Yeaveley), and GNP 704 (J. Allen, Roston). Duple coachwork is well represented, but GNP is a rare 1948 Plaxton-bodied forward-control conversion.
Richard Butler

the equivalent S-types. So it would continue with the D9s and D10s and the S-types up to the last S23. And, okay, I agree the LD8 Leylands were non-standard, as were the GD6 Guys, but the latter basically only ran from Dudley. The fleet never looked so unified after the LS18 Leopards and DD11 Fleetlines arrived in 1962/3.

While the fleet may have shown unity in design, it did not in condition. At the heart of this must have been an accountant, parsimoniously handing out pennies to engineers *pro rata* according to the numbers of vehicles on the allocation, and ignoring the terrain. Buses from the Birmingham garages operated through the cut-and-thrust of city traffic, and patch repairs to panels were commonplace, in marked contrast to well-maintained buses enjoying a serene existence in places like Hereford. Whilst creeping round the garages looking for something really ancient lurking at the back — after asking permission, of course, although it was handy that the engineers' offices were often nowhere near the entrance — we would look for the Head Office league table for accidents over the last month. Some tranquil spot like Banbury would always be basking in the golden glow of success at the top, while the poor old Birmingham garages would be occupying positions near the floor.

Conductors were supposed to clip a hole in your 'Day Anywhere' ticket, and you were mightily disappointed when one would hand it back with a grunt but no additional ventilation. A plea sometimes had the right effect, because there was nothing more satisfying after a long day than to count up the holes. Those days really could be long, too — particularly the 'day' we rode a late-evening bus into Leamington, Myton Road garage just before midnight, spotting the allocation before walking to Stephen's new family home in Myton (my first encounter with the joys of domestic central heating, incidentally).

Unfortunately, I recorded the buses used on a 'Day Anywhere' wandering only once. The details on page 7 show a Leicestershire-inclined marathon undertaken on Sunday 12 July 1964, one of our last outings. The first feature to strike one today is the ease of interchange from one route to another, even on a Sunday — just time to cruise the garage where applicable, and then away. And, yes, they all turned up. The second feature is the vehicle age profile. The oldest buses ridden that day were built in 1960, so all the drivers were free from the rigours of the manual gearbox. Midland Red worked its newest buses as hard as possible, and a Sunday 'Day Anywhere' meant you were unlikely to encounter older buses in service. Imagine our surprise in June 1965 when we enjoyed 17-year-old S8 3268, by then very much a survivor of the early postwar generation, working the 872 between Stafford and Newport, on a Sunday — an event illustrated in Mike Greenwood's *Glory Days: Midland Red*. The end of the era that particularly engaged us was in sight, and clearly we recognised that sort of opportunity would not occur again, because the trip was our swansong as far as 'Days Anywhere' were concerned. We had realised that Midland Red could get along fine without our taking down the number of every one we saw (actually it couldn't — the company's decline accelerated when I stopped spotting them). Work was crowding our spare time, which needed to be used for other things that occupy teenage minds, like girls — a matter which had to be addressed, and a 'Day Anywhere' ticket was not proving the way to do it . . .

Service	Origin	Destination	Vehicle	
153	0720 Shirley	0743 Birmingham bus station	D9	4967
X12	0757 Birmingham bus station	0831 Sutton (Parade)	LS18A	5176
X99	0854 Sutton (Parade)	0921 Tamworth bus station	LS18A	5190
765	0940 Tamworth bus station	1005 Lichfield bus station	LS18	5147
112	1100 Lichfield bus garage	1140 Burton (New St Park)	LS18	5227
703	1215 Burton (Wetmore Park)	1238 Swadlincote bus station	D9	5371
704	1308 Swadlincote bus station	1328 Ashby (The Green)	D9	5333
668	1348 Ashby (Market St)	1410 Coalville (Memorial Sq)	LS18	5208
669	1440 Coalville (Memorial Sq)	1520 Leicester (St Margaret's)	D9	5357
L8	1635 Leicester (St Margaret's)	1705 South Wigston	DD11	5267
L8	1725 South Wigston	1740 Leicester (Newarke St)	DD11	5250
658	1830 Leicester (The Newarke)	1915 Hinckley bus garage	D9	5318
658	1935 Hinckley bus garage	1955 Nuneaton bus station	D9	4989
658	2035 Nuneaton bus station	2110 Coventry (Pool Meadow)	D9	5007
159	2120 Coventry (Pool Meadow)	2218 Birmingham bus station	D9	4849
154	2230 Birmingham bus station	2253 Shirley	D9	4849

It is inevitable that this type of book should concentrate on the operations and vehicles but it should never be forgotten that the vast Midland Red network of buses scurrying to and fro was the result of the efforts of thousands of employees, the overwhelming majority of whom were dedicated to their job and including many who devoted their entire working lives to the company.

The text often mentions service frequencies to give the reader some idea of the nature of the routes concerned. The book basically covers the 1945-70 period, and the pedantic timetable buff should note that, during this time, frequencies increased and decreased from those quoted as demand changed. Indeed, some of the routes were highly seasonal, and frequencies varied from summer to winter, when I was less likely to encounter them. So settle back, pretend you're on a dual-purpose BMMO, and over the following pages, in a clockwise direction around the network, enjoy some Midland Red days.

Far left: A very early post-World War 2 scene, probably 1946, at Worcester's Newport Street bus station. SOS CON-type 1526 (HA 9477) of 1934 leads a 1936 SON-type, that year's deliveries being distinguishable by their sliding entrance doors. The SON was the first type with Midland Red's own diesel engine, following the previous year's DON model with AEC 7.7-litre diesel engine. No 1526 was originally a petrol ON model, being reclassified CON when converted to diesel, making it very similar to the SONs. It has received a repaint, but the SON remains in wartime garb with camouflage roof. The war had caused a backlog in repainting; a contemporary *Staff Bulletin* recorded that 1,090 vehicles were repainted in 1947. *Ian Allan Library*

Left: No 1526 again, this time outside Ludlow garage, showing the changes brought by the extensive body rebuilding programme after the war. Most noticeably the half-drop ventilators in recessed window pans have been replaced by flush glazing with top sliders; the hint of a rain deflector above the vents was, however, unusual for these rebuilds. The moulded belt rail has also given way to plain panelling. The body rebuild enabled 1526 to last until 1955. LD8 class 4065, actually one of Leamington's allocation of these Leylands, stands behind after working the X35. *A. B. Cross*

Midland Red
– A Brief History

Below: Developing days of Midland Red, with 1920 Tilling-Stevens TS3 OH 1224. Even at this early date the 32-seat bodies were to the company's design, and were constructed by several builders, in this case Strachan & Brown. After around 10 years, this vehicle would be one of those which received the original body from an SOS Standard type that had been rebodied. It would then run until 1932.
BaMMOT Collection

The Birmingham & Midland Motor Omnibus Company Ltd (BMMO) was registered on 26 November 1904, and became part of the vast British Electric Traction (BET) empire the following year. It reverted entirely to horse buses in 1907, despite the company name, but resumed motorbus operation in Birmingham with Tilling-Stevens vehicles from 1912. In 1914 Birmingham Corporation and BMMO entered into an agreement whereby the company continued to operate services between Birmingham and places outside the city boundary but agreed to leave the operation of city services entirely to the Corporation, which, in turn, agreed not to compete outside the Birmingham boundary. The company, which became familiarly known as Midland Red, then began a rapid growth, including the replacement of tramways of Midland Red's sister companies in BET, and became the largest bus operator outside London in England and Wales.

This success was threatened in the early 1920s by small firms using fast, light small buses. Midland Red's Chief Engineer, Mr L. G. Wyndham Shire, wanted buses that had the same performance characteristics as those of its competitors, but with the carrying capacity of the Tillings. The market place could not provide, so the company began to build its own buses. These carried the initials SOS (thought to mean 'Superior Omnibus Specification', although some claim the first word is actually 'Shire's'), until production ceased in 1940 for the duration of World War 2. An idiosyncratic appearance disguised the advanced nature of the continuously evolving SOS designs, and some were built for sister companies within BET. As diesel power took over from petrol units in new buses from the mid-1930s, Midland Red developed its own diesel (more correctly known at the time as 'compression-ignition') engine, which was remarkably compact, and allowed 38/39 seats in a single-decker of prewar maximum dimensions. This was known as the K (for 'Kidney') engine. It would be nice to record that it was named, Shire-fashion, after a designer called Sidney Kidney, but sadly it referred to the shape of the combustion chamber. Similarly, Shire horses are not an early design of the great man.

Mr Shire retired in 1940, and was replaced as Chief Engineer by Mr D. M. Sinclair, whose talents in unorthodox bus design had been honed at Northern General Transport. Postwar Midland Reds would share the ruggedness of their prewar counterparts, but look right up to date. Single-deckers re-entered production in 1946, all with underfloor engines and four years ahead of the big boys. Floor-height difficulties meant that double-deckers, for the time being, remained front-engined, but concealed radiators (to match the single-deckers) streamlined their appearance. The SOS name was dropped — buses became known as BMMO products, the initials of the company's official title. Mr Sinclair was determined that Midland Red passengers should have 'the finest buses in this or any other country' and, in 1949, set up 'bus design committees' to further that aim.

The success of the company was not due simply to its vehicles, but also the commercial wisdom of Traffic Manager Mr O. C. Power, under whose ægis, amongst many other initiatives, the 'Day Anywhere' ticket was originally introduced. Messrs Shire and Power had run the company without a general manager above them — only after Mr Power's death in harness in 1943 did Mr Sinclair become the first Midland Red General Manager.

The early postwar years saw petrol rationing for private cars, and a boom in bus travel. Over the four days of Whitsuntide 1947, Midland Red buses and coaches, then virtually unassisted by postwar deliveries, travelled 754,123 miles and carried 3,912,746 passengers. The average fare at the time was 3d (one quarter of 5p). The next few years saw the company introduce 200 entirely new services and well over 2,000 increases in service frequency. Youngsters can have no

Left: The Standard SOS was the first design of Midland Red chassis. HA 2424 was new in 1925, and was one of 51 rebuilt in 1929-30 to form the ODD class with new 26-seat bodies built entirely by United or assembled by Carlyle Works from parts supplied by United. They were later upseated to 30, and ran until the closing months of 1938. HA 2424 works a Malvern local service in 1936 while, behind, new FEDD BHA 326 has arrived from Birmingham on service 144. United is particularly known as a large bus operator in northeast England, but it also ran buses much further south along the eastern side of the country, until separated to form Eastern Counties. The bodybuilding facility also passed to the latter and was soon to be further split away as Eastern Coach Works.
R. T. Wilson, courtesy BaMMOT

idea of how mighty Midland Red was, operating nearly 1,900 buses and coaches, mostly constructed by itself. Setting aside the significant coaching activities, there were 1,200 stage-carriage services over a route mileage nearly 7,000 miles in length, in 15 counties covering 12,000 square miles. The company was big enough to form its own Symphony Orchestra and Male Voice Choir (later the Salon Orchestra and Singers), its own film unit, and to generate a wide range of social activities, mostly sporting but also including a horticultural society. The postwar growth and the backlog in vehicle replacements caused the company to supplement its own bus production with batches of double-deckers built by AEC, Guy and Leyland.

Two hefty increases in fuel tax began a spiral of fare increases from 1951 to counter rising costs. A steady decline in patronage set in from the mid-1950s, which was particularly critical for the many country services operated by the company. Pay rates could not compete with other industries, and, as the old-timers retired, by the late 1960s Midland Red was in a desperate state with staff shortages in all areas of activity, not least designers, craftsmen, engineers and platform staff. Replacement of the huge early postwar fleet had again seen outside vehicles purchased from 1962, in the form of Leyland Leopards and Daimler Fleetlines. These supplemented the company's falling output until BMMO production ceased in 1970, shortly after Mr Sinclair's retirement at the end of 1966 and BET's selling its bus interests to the state to become part of the National Bus

Company. The new West Midlands Passenger Transport Executive, formed in 1969, was required to integrate all public transport in its area, and those controlling the National Bus Company decided to sell Midland Red's West Midlands operations to the PTE for £3.6 million in 1973 rather than come to an operating agreement. No doubt the injection of capital was seen as a way to reinvest in the remainder of the company for the future, and the official title became Midland Red Omnibus Co Ltd in March 1974. But the loss of the West Midlands had left a company with a distinctly rural emphasis and, despite desperate service pruning, Midland Red simply died. It was divided, initially, into five pieces with effect from September 1981. These successor companies included 'Midland Red' in their titles and were subsequently privatised — two of them merging to leave four. All, however, are now in the hands of large groups, which cannot afford sentiment for their proud red heritage, adopting instead corporate liveries to convince their London bankers of their market penetration.

Another Ian Allan publication, *Glory Days: Midland Red*, by Mike Greenwood, gives much fuller information on the company. Its buses are fortunately preserved by a number of societies and individuals but the biggest collection of SOS and BMMO products can be found at the Birmingham & Midland Museum of Transport (BaMMOT) at Wythall, just off the A435 (M42 junction 3) to the south of Birmingham.

Around Birmingham

Bearwood garage, just within Smethwick with a corner of the premises actually in Birmingham, was for many years the headquarters of Midland Red. The B82 from Edmund Street, central Birmingham, via the Dudley Road actually passed the garage, but the quicker way was to catch service 9 along the Hagley Road to the 'King's Head' and walk up Bearwood Road. The B82, however, was rather interesting.

Midland Red service numbering had evolved so that all routes were numbered above 100, reaching almost 999, leaving the numbers below 100 for Birmingham Corporation. A number of towns had local services with an appropriate letter prefix, such as 'S' for Shrewsbury, Stourbridge, Stafford and Solihull, and numbers up to 99. B82 thus indicated a Birmingham local service, and was part of a group of services notionally jointly operated with the city's transport department. Joint operation of the Dudley Road corridor out of Birmingham and across the boundary into Smethwick had long been a feature; indeed, earlier in the century, BET-owned tramcars operated the long route through Oldbury to Dudley, and Birmingham Corporation worked the much shorter Bearwood and Soho routes which were an exception to the 1914 agreement restricting the Corporation's vehicles to within the city. The BET tramway leases in Smethwick, Oldbury, Rowley Regis and Tipton were purchased by the local authorities on 1 January 1939, whilst that within Dudley expired. Birmingham trams had actually taken over the Dudley route by agreement in *lieu* of the BET trams in 1928. The various local authorities beyond the Birmingham boundary, not being bus operators in their own right, came to an agreement with BET that Midland Red motorbuses should replace the tramways. Thus the Dudley Road group of services effectively reverted to the pre-1928 two-operator arrangements, but with Corporation and Company motorbuses. The conversion took place on 30 September 1939, bringing to an end tramway operation in the Black Country, despite the outbreak of war earlier that month, which, among other things, threatened the import of fuel, which the electric trams could have managed without.

The agreed mileages by each operator were carefully protected; in my era, at least, there were Corporation-worked B81 short workings between Bearwood and Windmill Lane on Fridays to maintain the balance. The Bearwood B82 was largely (but not entirely) Corporation-worked; short workings between the city centre and the boundary at Grove Lane, numbered B80, and the Soho B83 were completely so. A selection of numbers up to B89 indicated workings on the Dudley leg. These were almost entirely Midland Red, although a solitary Corporation morning-peak B85 (Spon Lane–Birmingham) was a photographer's collector's item! The Corporation workings passed to West Midlands PTE in 1969, and one of my early WMPTE duties was to supply a Midland Red opposite number with details of our lost mileage. He, in turn, supplied Midland Red's, which was always considerably greater. The accountants then calculated a financial adjustment. Our joint misery ceased when WMPTE acquired the Midland Red services in 1973.

The Birmingham City Transport buses, working out of Rosebery Street garage, always looked odd showing the 'B' prefix letter. This was exacerbated by Rosebery Street's vehicles, which were mostly well adrift from what might be regarded as the BCT standard. The initial replacements for the trams were torque-converter Leyland Titan TD6c buses, bodied by Leyland itself, with just a few nods towards BCT's ideas on styling. Their postwar replacements were largely taken from the batch of 50 Leyland Titan PD2s with Park Royal bodies displaying similar disregard for BCT design. Even the few Daimler COG5s which crept onto the allocation would include some 'weirdies', such as Manchester-style examples rebodied after war damage and No 1235 with its postwar prototype Brush body. Rosebery Street closed in 1968, and the prefix was dropped from both operators' vehicles; it was then Midland Red's buses which looked odd with only two-digit service numbers.

After the opening of Bearwood bus station in 1952, the B82 terminated there, opposite the 'King's Head'. Also to be seen there

Right: One of Birmingham's 1950 Park Royal-bodied Leyland Titan PD2s which figured prominently on the B82 route for around 18 years, No 2221 exits Herbert Road for Bearwood bus station in April 1968. *Paul Gray*

were the buses of West Bromwich Corporation. The services between West Bromwich and Bearwood were the first to be operated jointly by Midland Red and a municipality, an arrangement that began in April 1935. More were to follow.

The buses that rattled the windows of Midland Red's Bearwood premises were thus often Birmingham City Transport Leyland Titans on the B82. The assortment of buildings that made up Bearwood garage was heralded at street level by the three big enquiry-office windows with curved glass that must have been fearsomely expensive when installed in 1923. Interesting experimental vehicles could be found anywhere around the company's network, but most particularly at Bearwood. (A 1958 staff bulletin commented that 1,400 buses carried one or more experimental items, ranging from air-cooled engines to brake parts — in a fleet of just under 1,900 vehicles!). It seemed impossible to go through the area without seeing No 2541 (HHA 1), the D1 postwar prototype double-decker which, alongside the S1, spent most of its life at Bearwood. Various departmental vehicles would also be around, not least the Driving School fleet. This included, in my youth, two 1937 SLR coaches with full-width cabs which I thought were beautiful. One survived until 1963, just missing the era when people had sufficient money in their pockets to act on thoughts of preservation. They were replaced by equally-long-lived relegated C1 coaches, which also swept away other Driving School veterans such as SONs converted to full-width cabs for their later role.

The single word 'Bearwood' is enough to make the eyes of any Midland Red *aficionado* light up. Two more words — 'Carlyle Works' — have a similar effect. This was located in Carlyle Road, Edgbaston — a couple of miles down and just off the Hagley Road towards the centre of Birmingham.

Early SOS chassis were assembled at Bearwood. A substantial part of the Carlyle Road property had been bought from Daimler in 1920 and used for body overhauls and repair work. The remainder was purchased in November 1924, and, from early the next year, new chassis were assembled at Carlyle Works. Bearwood, however, retained the overhaul and refitting of bus chassis and engines, together with experimental work and some chassis assembly.

This splitting of overhaul work over two sites was plainly unsatisfactory, and in 1941 plans were prepared for a major reconstruction of Carlyle Works. World War 2 prevented immediate action, however, and postwar materials shortages meant progress was gradual and slow. Various parts of the plan were implemented until, in November 1954, the complex, then also known as Central Works, was relaunched as the most up-to-date vehicle overhaul works in the

Left: Most of the 65 CHA-registered SON-class single-deckers of 1936 had their English Electric bodies extensively rebuilt and ran for around 20 years. No 1927 (CHA 551), however, did not receive a body rebuild, and in 1951 was the first to be withdrawn. It reappeared the following year as a dual-control trainer, in which capacity it served the company's Driving School at Bearwood until 1962. This would have been a good preservation candidate because, apart from the full-width cab, the rest of the bus remained largely original. The infant movement was hampered, however, not only by lack of finance and accommodation, but also by Mr Sinclair's unsympathetic views on preserving the past. *G. H. Stone*

country — something of an understatement, as new bodies and chassis were assembled on the site too. The chassis-production building had capacity in excess of Midland Red's requirements but, alas, the potential for sales to other companies was never realised, despite some demonstration loans of S15-class buses to sister BET-group operators. The old hands continued to call Central Works 'Carlyle', which led to at least one unfortunate incident. A new driver at Leamington was instructed to take an LD8 double-decker to Carlyle Works. Some hours later the Works phoned Leamington's resident man-in-a-white-coat, asking why the expected bus had not been delivered. The answer to the puzzle was provided by the next phone call, this time from the missing driver. He was seeking instructions as he had not been able to reach Carlisle, because the bus had run out of fuel just north of Preston!

My father found a contact within Midland Red who fixed up a tour of Central Works for my friend Peter and me in 1960 — this was the only time I recall my father responding to my bus interest, and I suspect he had visions of my becoming a BET trainee when I left school. Instead he left home and I joined Birmingham City Transport in 1965, but that's another story. Our 1960 visit was certainly a Midland Red day to remember, because, whereas a kid could slip unnoticed into any of the garages, Central Works had a security reputation akin to that of Colditz.

Birmingham (Digbeth) and Stourbridge garages also incorporated coach or bus stations respectively, which must have seemed a good

Above: BMMO D9s under construction at Central Works in 1960. *Ian Allan Library*

wonderful new insight. C5 coaches were still being built, some to motorway specification. The first D9 buses had just come into service and 4871, now preserved at Wythall, was almost ready for the road. Behind it were more D9s in less and less advanced state as you went down the line. This caused a number-spotting crisis — how many of them could you class as seen when some were simply frames?

The Experimental & Development Department held the biggest surprises, however. We hoped that a company as innovative as Midland Red would have such a section, staffed by absent-minded boffins in odd socks, whose strokes of genius would be test-piloted by dashing ex-RAF types who knew no fear, and had a delicious damsel waiting outside the main gate, pouting and stretched across the seat of an open sports car. We held dreams of a really exciting, secret new bus tucked away and we were not to be disappointed, except in the damsel department. Our anticipation was cranked up by the sight of an S8 extended to an extraordinary 45ft in length, which seemed a strange thing to do, and our guide would not explain it! We subsequently learned it was an endeavour to persuade the Ministry of Transport that longer vehicles were practical. The idea of going to extremes obviously worked, because 36ft-long vehicles were permitted from the following year. (One can imagine a nervous boffin, anxiously cleaning his specs on his white coat, explaining to the BMMO chief test pilot that this monster needed to be threaded through the congested streets of central London and receiving a booming reply, Kenneth More-fashion: 'What! Only 45ft long? Piece of cake, old sport!') Then, with a theatrical flourish, a huge door was slid back a few inches, and we were invited inside. There was 4943, the first of the company's two D10s, virtually complete. The two D10s represented the highest point of BMMO technology, and were the only underfloor-engined double-deckers to operate successfully on British roads until, a quarter of a century later, Volvo managed to produce a similar configuration. Peter and I imagined hundreds of D10s on the road; we certainly never thought that BMMO production would cease only 10 years later.

idea at the time. Waiting passengers, none too reassuringly, were sometimes able to gaze over accident-damaged vehicles awaiting assessment of repairs. Central Works Body Shop was the destination of the worst of these. Many of the 50 buses in there were routine body overhauls, but, amongst the repairs, we gazed in awe at one S14 with only the rear end remaining after what must have been a horrifying accident. Overhauled buses passed along to the paint shop, the spray plant being revolutionary when first constructed. This was all much more absorbing to me than the chassis-overhaul department, but Peter, being mechanically minded, took great interest in the rows of axles, gearboxes, springs, steering gear etc plus engines in the engine shop. These vital parts do not have the same fascination for me when separated from the vehicle — like clothes without a person wearing them.

Seeing new buses and coaches under construction provided a

Handily situated adjacent to Central Works, but on Vernon Road, was Midland House, a former private hospital built in the 1860s and bought by the company for use as offices. Following its opening in 1953, it became the registered offices of Midland Red. Many departments transferred from Bearwood to Midland House and Central Works at this time, and Bearwood's responsibilities reduced considerably. After the big transfer of services to WMPTE took place in December 1973, men without souls closed Bearwood, and it was demolished soon after. When the company was dismantled in 1981

Left: The extraordinary 45ft-long S8 seen at Central Works in 1960; the last 15ft is clearly a temporary structure. Metro-Cammell-bodied 3220 started life in 1948 as a 40-seater, being lengthened to nearly 30ft to take advantage of relaxed vehicle dimensions, allowing 44 seats in a programme which covered all of the S6/8/9/10/11 classes between 1951 and 1953. It reverted to normal after its 1960 adventure and ran until 1965.
Maurice Norton

more men without souls endeavoured to close Carlyle (Central) Works, but it lived on for a time, particularly as the birthplace of van-derived minibuses which carried the name Carlyle to operators across the country. I can't imagine what Mr Sinclair would have thought of his Central Works making buses out of delivery vans, but it didn't last and the complex was finally closed and sold for housing. The men with calculators where their hearts might have been were no doubt right, but it is sad anyway.

Another important Midland Red property in Birmingham was in Digbeth, a short walk from the famous Bull Ring. Digbeth, as mentioned earlier, combined a garage with a coach station. The company's coach fleet remained immaculate, and I do mean immaculate, until the mid-1960s. Amongst the consequences of the severe shortage of engineering staff from then on was the use of tour coaches on bus services. This desperate act ruined prestige vehicles

on work for which they were totally unsuited, even if their appearance on peak-time local services did give me the opportunity to ride on a CL2-class Scottish tour coach at last! I shall not waste ink on the dreadful white National coach livery, which followed soon after.

Digbeth had the largest allocation of buses in the fleet, and the garage always needed a yard in the vicinity to accommodate the overflow. This yard regularly changed location as inner Birmingham was redeveloped. In the mid-1950s Digbeth's allocation numbered nearly 120 vehicles, despite the transfer in 1951 of 34 buses to another fairly central garage in Sheepcote Street, acquired from British Road Services.

Looking around Digbeth was never a problem, because, as a coach station, it was wide-open to the public and the maintenance areas were clearly visible. There was rarely anything new for me to see, however, because Digbeth ran my local services. These terminated in a cluster beneath St Martin's Church in the old Bull Ring. Other important Midland Red termini were Station Street, New Street, Navigation Street and Edmund Street, the last-mentioned accommodating the notionally jointly-operated services with Birmingham City Transport along Dudley Road. The rebuilding of the Bull Ring gave our services a peripatetic existence until the opening of Midland Red's under-cover bus station on 1 November 1963. This brought all the company's services under one roof, except those in Edmund Street. It formed part of the new Bull Ring development and, in retrospect, can now be seen as the last great event for this wonderful company. Midland Red thought it was meeting the best needs of its passengers by providing the under-cover interchange for nearly all its Birmingham services, just as the City Fathers meant well with the whole of the Bull Ring redevelopment. It proved a flawed concept, however, paralleling the fortunes of the wider Bull Ring project. The bus station suffered badly from diesel fumes, poor lighting and condensation, and quickly took on a seedy appearance. As the company began to dissolve from 1973, successor operators found excuses to withdraw their services from the place. Eventually, basically only Midland Red West remained there, and the loneliness was worse than the fumes.

Right: Journey's end for the author on the Stratford Road at Robin Hood Island, Hall Green, Birmingham. Birmingham City Transport 1864 was one of many 1948 Metro-Cammell-bodied Daimler CVG6 buses allocated to Highgate Road garage, which, until its 1962 closure, worked the 37 service. The Midland Red D7, behind in this June 1960 view, would cross the boundary to Shirley (where the writer would have to travel if using a 'Day Anywhere' ticket) *en route* to Solihull. The 37 and 154 are now combined as today's service 6. The D7 is Digbeth's 4482, now preserved at Wythall. *A. B. Cross*

Through the Black Country to Stafford

A 'Day Anywhere' to Stafford was a good opportunity to include an exploration of the Black Country. The towns of Walsall, West Bromwich and Wolverhampton, however, had their own Corporation bus services, including joint services between each other, which meant that Midland Red services were relatively thin to the north of West Bromwich, Wednesbury and Bilston. Dudley, and towns to the south, were firmly in the hands of Midland Red. The three municipal operators, along with Birmingham City Transport, were merged to form the West Midlands Passenger Transport Executive in 1969. The PTE purchased Midland Red's local services in its area in 1973, and it was astonishing to see the Dudley stronghold change entirely to the PTE's blue and cream. Only the X96 family of services into Dudley survived, and they were soon diverted away via the motorway.

To head towards Wolverhampton, one could go via West Bromwich on the Corporation buses or via Dudley on the Midland Red. West Bromwich buses remained clad in a beautifully-lined-out livery, with shaded lettering, in a manner abandoned almost everywhere else on the grounds of economy, yet West Brom could boast the cheapest fares in the area. The West Bromwich Corporation Act of 1900 had given the Corporation powers to operate tramcars, but this right was never exercised. Existing tramways were purchased by the Corporation in 1902, electrified, and then leased back to the companies. The lease with South Staffordshire Tramways expired in 1924, and an agreement was reached with Birmingham Corporation Tramways for its tramcars to work the mileage in *lieu*. The Spon Lane and Bromford Lane tramways, for so long the preserve of the Birmingham & Midland Tramways, were replaced by West Bromwich motorbuses in November 1929. Bus services had been established after a shaky start, with Tilling-Stevens (1919-26), Guy (1927-9) and then Dennis vehicles being favoured until 1936. The first diesel bus was a Daimler COG5 received in 1934. This manufacturer became the principal choice from 1936, the combination of Daimler chassis and Metro-Cammell bodies being firmly entrenched until shortly before the 1969 PTE takeover, by which time the Corporation had begun looking elsewhere for its bodywork.

West Bromwich's first joint route was to Walsall, operated from 1926 by motorbuses of both towns. Subsequent joint operations included to Aldridge and Streetly with Walsall Corporation, to Wolverhampton with that town's transport department, and a group of services into Smethwick (including Bearwood) worked jointly with Midland Red. A further joint arrangement with Midland Red was introduced as late as 1967. The tramways from Birmingham, through the borough to Wednesbury and Dudley, were replaced by motorbuses in April 1939. Birmingham had worked these services entirely since 1924, but upon conversion they became a joint Birmingham/West Bromwich operation, reflecting the mileage in each borough.

The Midland Red 'Day Anywhere' ticket user would generally travel via Dudley rather than West Bromwich, employing any one of a number of routes. The Black Country is a series of villages that have grown together, resulting in the need to serve a variety of flows rather than provide strong corridor bus routes with close frequencies. This exacerbated Midland Red's tendency to try and serve every road, and gave rise to a network of considerable complexity over terrain that could be challenging to earlier generations of buses, especially around Dudley itself. These routes were worked from several garages, all now closed.

Many stops in the Black Country were provided with lay-bys to assist the general traffic flow but, at the same time, ensured the Midland Red driver was trapped until a gap appeared. Maintenance

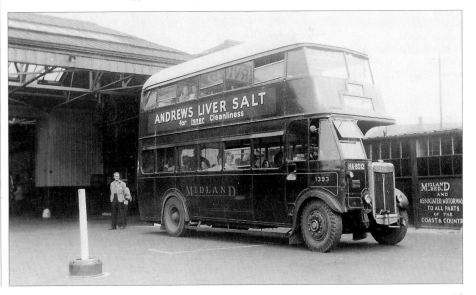

Below: The 50 rear-entrance double-deckers built in 1932, and later familiarly known as the REDD class, had quite long lives, running until 1948-51. They were particularly associated with the Leicester area, having concentrated there by 1940 after FEDD vehicles had taken over in other areas. They later began to spread further afield again as Leicester received newer stock, and 1393 (HA 8012) is seen working Stourbridge local route S50 to The Heath from the forecourt of the town's garage, which continued to be a departure point for certain services after it was absorbed into an extension of the garage. No 1393 was bodied by Short Bros, but Eastern Counties, Brush and Metro-Cammell were also involved in the body contracts.
Malcolm Keeley Collection

of these lay-bys seemed to be non-existent, so, by the time of the D9s, potholes were numerous. Additionally, they were separated from the highway proper by slightly raised kerbing. The D9, with its set-back front axle, was a bouncy beast at the best of times. Of course, they entered the lay-by at an angle, so each of the four wheels would encounter the kerbing at a different time. The bus would therefore be bouncing all over the place, before dropping into the random selection of potholes. At least the driver had the steering wheel to hang on to, unlike the mass of bodies thrown about the upper deck!

Dudley was, for many years, a curiosity, being an island of Worcestershire completely surrounded by Staffordshire. It had an extensive bus station, opened in 1952, perched on a steep incline,

which summed up the topography of the area. The bus station, to the outsider, was surely the place to catch a bus to Wolverhampton — a Midland Red, of course. There was another important route, however, its terminus hidden away in Stone Street, behind the Market Place. This was Wolverhampton Corporation's service 58 (8B in earlier times), for 40 years until 1967 run with *trolleybuses* — a fact to which I was oblivious until the motorbus replacement programme was announced.

Wolverhampton Corporation was an early and enthusiastic operator of trolleybuses, first introducing them in 1923 on the Wednesfield route, and by 1928 it had not only replaced its own tramways but also purchased BET-owned company lines for immediate trolleybus substitution. Expansion of the trolleybus fleet continued in the early 1930s, when the electric vehicles replaced motorbuses on some routes. The Corporation's motorbus services had developed in an interesting fashion, including the adoption of a number of comparatively long routes in the 1920s following agreements with Midland Red and the Great Western Railway. The town was the home of the much-respected vehicle manufacturer Guy Motors, the buses and trolleybuses of which began to feature in Corporation orders from 1925, and which eventually became the principal source of supply. Daimler motorbuses, however, were first purchased in 1934 and regularly featured in deliveries until 1950, by which time most of the prewar fleet had been replaced by postwar buses and trolleybuses. Wartime buses and trolleybuses carried on, and most were rebodied in 1951/2. Rebodying of the earliest postwar trolleybuses took place between 1958 and 1962, but by this time the first conversion to motorbuses had occurred, achieved with the assistance of loaned Birmingham City Transport Daimlers. The conversion programme began in earnest in 1963 and ended with the long route to Dudley in March 1967, leaving the Corporation with a fleet of around 300 buses, mostly Guy Arabs, which passed to the PTE in 1969.

Midland Red had premises in Wolverhampton, and at one time its double-decker allocation was 100% Leyland, comprising wartime TD7 models and recently-delivered LD8s. A large new depot opened in 1964, capable of holding twice the 30 or so vehicles allocated, but sadly the decline in the company's fortunes meant it closed in 1971. While the territorial deals agreed between Wolverhampton Corporation and Midland Red meant that the Corporation ran several rural routes to the north and west of the town, the route north to Stafford was Midland Red's. Passengers on the through Birmingham–Wolverhampton–Stafford services had to re-book in Wolverhampton, however, so that the Corporation could be credited with the revenue due to it under the agreements. One wonders what financial arrangements were made for 'Day Anywhere' ticket-holders, who were blissfully unaware of the inconvenience of re-booking.

Midland Red had another garage at Stafford, where the principal interest for some years was the two D10s, which spent most of their lives there. It was, however, a border town, with the bus services of sister BET company Potteries Motor Traction being included in the Midland Red timetable book. PMT's main activities were, it will not be a shock to reveal, in the Potteries. The company's origins were in BET subsidiary Potteries Electric Traction, the tramcars of which, like those in the Black Country, began to be overwhelmed by competing motorbuses in the 1920s. The solution was remarkably similar, with the company replacing its trams with SOS buses by 1928. Midland Red's SOS products continued to be purchased until 1933, but then Leyland became principal supplier. PMT followed a policy of buying up the competition, and the fleet generally contained significant numbers of buses from purchased operators. The vehicle stock acquired in this way during the early postwar years often had substandard bodywork, and this encouraged substantial rebuilding and rebodying exercises, adding to the interest of the fleet.

The route back towards Birmingham could be taken via Walsall. Walsall Corporation bus operations were more like those of a company than a municipal operator, and its vehicles ranged well beyond the town's boundaries. Deals with Midland Red resulted in 1949 in a half-hourly, jointly-operated Stafford–Cannock–Bloxwich–Walsall–Dudley service (Midland Red 865; Walsall 65). Dennis had been the dominant choice for Walsall buses until the outbreak of war in 1939, but the allocation of Guy Arabs during the war led to this model's becoming standard until 1951, when Leylands began to feature. Walsall's fleet of buses and trolleybuses became legendary in the 1950s and '60s for their variety and the number of conversion jobs. Add to this occasional secondhand purchases and a tendency to re-mount windows in white glazing rubber, and you had a fleet that was interesting but not very easy on the eye. This was the

Below: The 150 FEDDs built in 1938/9 had bodies by Brush — not so dainty but just as full of character. The body construction reverted to a timber frame and was not as robust, needing a major reconstruction programme between 1949 and 1951.
FHA 229, however, is seen here looking splendid when new. Behind is Midland Red's Dudley garage at the foot of Castle Hill (the site is now a traffic island). A Bundy time-recording clock for Birmingham City Transport crews is to the side. FHA 229, later given fleetnumber 2247, is working service 246, known as the D & S (Dudley & Stourbridge), echoing the name of the former tramway company.
The Omnibus Society

Right: FEDD 2254 (FHA 236) of 1939 shows the effect of postwar body rebuilding with rubber mounted flush glazing on the side windows. The Brush body is of further interest, however, because it was classed as experimental when new, and had the more rounded proportions of the last batch of FEDDs, FHA 836-85. This cluster of Midland Red buses at Stourbridge Town railway station, one of three bus termini in the vicinity of the station including the company's garage, shows the FEDD working local service S56 to Norton Estate; AD2-class AEC Regent II 3147 stands alongside, while a BMMO D5B loads in the background. No 2254 was amongst the last six FEDDs, being withdrawn at the end of November 1960 with 2219/28 and 2358/72/81. *Tennent's Trains, Halesowen*

The 100 underfloor-engined BMMO S6 buses were years ahead of their time when built in 1946/7. The lengthening undertaken at the rear end of all the 1946-50 single-deckers to gain an extra row of seats improved the balance of the design, removing the short-tailed look. A tweak to the front windscreen on the 8ft-wide models (S8 onwards) completed a design classic. The S6s were originally to be numbered 2601-2700, more or less following on from the fleetnumbers allocated to the existing fleet in 1944, hence the registration numbers HHA 601-700. In the event their numbers commenced at 3000. No 3010 was bodied by Metro-Cammell, which shared early postwar contracts with Brush, all to BMMO design. It is seen in Bridgnorth Road, Wollaston, Stourbridge, on service 190, an indirect route from Birmingham to Ludlow taking over three hours, compared to the 2½ hours of service 192 via Kidderminster. The 190 ran every two hours on weekdays and hourly at weekends between Birmingham, Stourbridge, Kinver and Bridgnorth, with certain journeys extended to Ludlow over two services acquired from Corvedale of Ludlow in 1953 — the 971 via Weston and 972 via Wenlock Edge.
Tennent's Trains, Halesowen

Above: The construction of buses by the company was interrupted by World War 2. A surprising allocation by the authorities to Midland Red in 1942 was of six AEC Regents with Brush bodies, originally intended for Coventry Corporation, where need was surely greater. Although to peacetime design, the bodies needed extensive reconstruction in 1951, as seen here on 2441 (GHA 795) at Dudley bus station. Behind, looking very different, but actually mechanically virtually identical, with its AEC 7.7-litre engine and crash gearbox, is a 1948 AD2-class AEC Regent II, also with Brush body but to Mr Sinclair's sleek postwar design. The six wartime Regents ran until 1954/5, almost entirely from Harts Hill garage in Brierley Hill. *G. H. Stone*

period when Ronald Edgley Cox ran the undertaking — there is a book to be written about this man, but no-one has been bold enough to do it yet! Needless to say, Midland Red 'Day Anywhere' tickets were not valid on Walsall-worked journeys on the Stafford service, and I remember having to pay to travel on one of Edgley Cox's ghastly Daimler Fleetlines, which contrived to seat 70 unfortunates within the shorter length he specified, after he had lengthened several earlier vehicles.

Trolleybuses had been first introduced to Walsall on the service to Wolverhampton via Willenhall. This was worked by both Corporations, and thus became one of the few joint operations of trolleybuses in Britain. More trolleybuses replaced the last tramcars to Bloxwich, in 1933. Mr Edgley Cox favoured trolleybuses, and expanded this core network until 1963, when the trolleybus fleet reached its maximum of 61. Fleet and infrastructure renewals were achieved cheaply by purchasing secondhand equipment from other trolleybus systems being closed down. Wolverhampton's decision to replace its trolleybuses, and the promise of major dislocation caused by motorway construction, led to the conversion of the joint service in 1965. No other conversions were planned before absorption into West Midlands PTE, and one can only speculate when the network would have closed, if ever, without the takeover.

Midland Red possessed comparatively few routes of significant frequency, but the 118 Birmingham–Walsall service was one of them. In early postwar years it boasted a 6-7min headway, decreasing only on Sunday mornings to a 15min frequency. This was not all, because, between each 118 at the Birmingham end, there was either a 119 short working to and from the 'Scott Arms', Great Barr, or a 188 journey branching to and from Beeches Estate. For some years, four garages contributed buses to this group of services.

Boundary changes sometimes left the 1914 agreement with Birmingham Corporation behind, and the company found itself the sole supplier of bus services to developed areas now within Birmingham. The Walsall Road corridor (and also the College Road to New Oscott, immediately to the east) was the most significant of these instances, when the Urban District of Perry Barr was absorbed into the City of Birmingham in 1928, leaving only the section between Walsall and the 'Scott Arms' outside the Birmingham boundary. A new agreement between Birmingham Corporation and Midland Red, additional to the existing 1914 agreement, arranged that, until further notice, Midland Red would continue to provide the services and pass a mileage-based proportion of the net profits to the Corporation. In those parts of the city where Midland Red continued to provide bus services, but now on behalf of the Corporation, BCT fare scales were applied and BCT's standard round 'lollipop'-shaped bus stops were erected. These differed from stops elsewhere in the city, where company buses paralleled BCT services and stop plates carried the legend 'MIDLAND "RED" BUSES STOP HERE'. The latter were replaced in the 1950s by Midland Red wheel-and-tyre plates to the round BCT shape. In 1957/8, however, the 188, 119 and New Oscott short workings on the College Road corridor became services 52, 51 and 42 of Birmingham City Transport. A number of staff transferred with the services, but no vehicles were involved. This left Midland Red with only the 118 on the Walsall Road, although, for a time, Birmingham and Walsall were also linked by a limited-stop service, the X8. In the 1960s the 118 became a joint operation with Walsall Corporation, whose share passed to the PTE in 1969, and then, after the 1973 sale, it became entirely a PTE service. The PTE absorbed it into an extended 51 service to Walsall, ending any identification with what had once been an important Midland Red artery.

After Stafford, an alternative to the excitement of Walsall was to change buses at Cannock. One could reach Cannock either by bailing out of one's 65/865 or by travelling there on service 836. Midland Red operation in Cannock was actually very small until the 1973/4 takeovers of the original Green Bus of Rugeley and Harper Bros of

Heath Hayes. It did run service 104 to Birmingham from Cannock, but this went via Sutton Coldfield, took 85min and only ran every two hours, which was no doubt the reason I ended up on one of Edgley Cox's Fleetlines. For many years Harper Bros' principal service ran from Cannock via Aldridge to Kingstanding, where one could connect with frequent Birmingham City Transport buses, but

from June 1965 the Harper route was at last allowed into central Birmingham as a limited-stop service. Ironically, after the PTE bought out most Midland Red services into Birmingham in 1973, it was this money that Midland Red used to buy Harper Bros, thus adding this Birmingham service to its portfolio.

Right: The GD6 class comprised 20 Guy Arab III buses with Park Royal-framed Guy bodies purchased in 1949 to supplement new BMMO production. They did not, in any way, follow BMMO design standards and originally had powerful Meadows 10.35-litre engines, which made them a logical choice for Dudley garage's hilly territory. The Meadows units as fitted in the Arab were awkward to work on, leading to excessive downtime, so they were replaced as early as 1952 by BMMO 8-litre engines, which produced a unique combination but took the edge off their performance! No 3560 is seen at the terminus on Russells Hall Estate in April 1960.
Peter G. Smith

Right: The unpredictable adds interest to large fleets. The GD6 class was only ever allocated to Dudley, although day loans occurred and a few entered the engineering float and briefly worked elsewhere. GD6 3557 makes an unexpected appearance on Stourbridge local service S51 in High Street, Wollaston.
Tennent's Trains, Halesowen

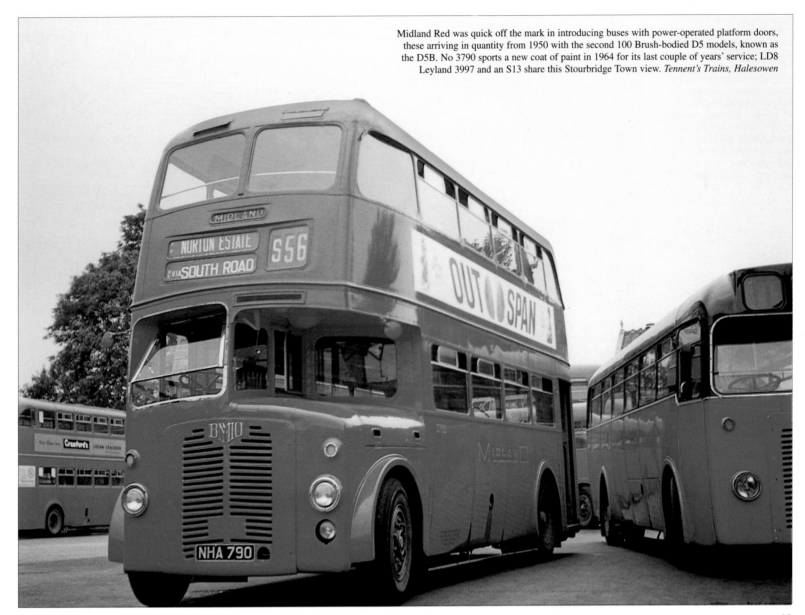

Midland Red was quick off the mark in introducing buses with power-operated platform doors, these arriving in quantity from 1950 with the second 100 Brush-bodied D5 models, known as the D5B. No 3790 sports a new coat of paint in 1964 for its last couple of years' service; LD8 Leyland 3997 and an S13 share this Stourbridge Town view. *Tennent's Trains, Halesowen*

Right: The single-deck equivalent of the FEDD was the ON family, of which the SON variant was built from 1936 to 1940, when war caused production to cease. No 2297 (FHA 452) was a 1939 delivery, and is seen loading on a 118 short working from Walsall bus station to Six Ways, Aston, before its Brush body was rebuilt in 1950; it was retired in 1958. Note that Mr Sinclair had the SOS radiator badges on the prewar buses replaced by BMMO. *R. A. Mills*

Below left & right: Midland Red received significant numbers of wartime Daimler CWA6 and Guy Arab austerity buses. The bodies on all the Daimlers and most of the Guys were constructed of unseasoned timber, and required extensive reconstruction by 1950/1. The company also took the opportunity to 'modernise' the front ends with built-up front wings — an improvement of dubious merit, and postwar destination indicators; sadly the FEDD and CON/DON/SON rebuilds were not blessed in this respect. Apart from the 1949 prototype rebuilds at Carlyle Works, the Daimlers' bodies were reconstructed by Willowbrook, and the Guys by Brush. Both types could be seen on the 118, the Daimlers being provided by Digbeth (Sheepcote Street after its opening in 1951) and the Guys by Sutton Coldfield garage. Daimler 2516 (GHA 940) is seen in High Street, Birmingham, awaiting its next departure time from New Street, whilst Guy 2581 (HHA 58) loiters for the same reason at the Walsall end. *R. T. Wilson, courtesy BaMMOT; Roy Marshall*

Left: The hourly 268 Wolverhampton–Coseley–Princes End service became one of the few Midland Red routes into central West Bromwich when, in 1967, it was extended through Great Bridge, Greets Green, across the centre of West Bromwich to Stone Cross and the town's Yew Tree Estate as a joint service with the Corporation's 2/2T route. The two operators jointly provided what was basically a 15min service between Great Bridge and Yew Tree. The 220/1 were much longer established joint Midland Red/West Bromwich routes between the town and Bearwood. Each operated half-hourly, the 220 increasing to 20min and the 221 to 15min on Saturdays. This scene in West Bromwich centre shows Wolverhampton-allocated 1961 BMMO D9 4928 overtaking West Bromwich's first 30ft-long double-decker, 1958 Daimler CVG6LX-30/Metro-Cammell 214, on 20 September 1969. At the end of the month 214 would become a WMPTE bus. *Maurice Collignon*

Left: The arrival of five ex-Sheffield 1960 Leyland Leopard L1s with Weymann Fanfare 41-seat coach bodies for bus use in 1970 led to speculation that large numbers of secondhand vehicles would follow to ease the shortage of roadworthy buses. It was not to be, however, and the Leopards lasted only until 1971. No 6259 (6173 WJ) is seen on Hagley Road West, alongside Bearwood bus station, working Wolverhampton–Dudley–Birmingham service 126 in April 1971. The bus fleet would see more secondhand buses during the decade due to takeovers, but not until the 1980s would buying used vehicles become regular policy. *E. V. Trigg*

Above: The 100 1952/3 LD8-class buses were standard Leyland-bodied Leyland PD2/12 models modified to suit Midland Red's ideas on styling. The LD8s and early D7s all suffered from having their window glazing rubbers being sprayed red when that method of painting was first introduced; better masking prevented later vehicles' being similarly spoilt. Looking well laden but scruffy, LD8 3993 is hard at work in New Road, Halesowen, in 1966, having just descended Mucklow Hill. Upon rounding the first bend at the top of the hill, passengers are rewarded with a grand vista over Worcestershire and Shropshire, with the Clent Hills in the near distance. The mile-long hill includes maximum gradients of 1 in 9, so, while buses struggled uphill, drivers travelling downwards had to treat the gradient with respect in the days before air brakes. I was aboard a D9 — a model notorious for poor braking, after the disc brakes were removed — travelling down the hill at maximum speed, when the driver changed down to third to assist pulling it up for the stop and traffic island at the bottom. The consequences for both engine and gearbox were disastrous. *Tennent's Trains, Halesowen*

Left: The last 143 BMMO single-deckers, 5849-5991, were originally announced as further S17 models but, in practice, employed a modified bodyshell with longer windows, offside emergency door and a variety of ventilation and seating qualities to create the S21, S22 and S23 classes. The S21s were 30 49-seat semi-coaches built in 1967. When new, 5849-59 had black roofs, but 5860-78 reflected a change of policy by featuring maroon roofs. Probably all had been simplified to all-over red by the time 5866 was seen in Rugeley on the 825 Lichfield–Stafford service on 17 March 1973. *Richard Butler*

Right: Very typical of Wolverhampton's early postwar trolleybuses was 619 with its 8ft-wide Park Royal body mounted on Guy BT or, as in this case, Sunbeam F4 chassis. It is seen bound for Dudley in 1960. *T. W. Moore*

Right: Loyal to Guys produced in the town, Wolverhampton Corporation nevertheless showed hints of an AEC tendency in the 1960s. Between a batch of AEC-engined Guy Arab Vs and half a dozen AEC Swifts came five AEC Renowns with MCW 72-seat bodies in 1966, including 185 seen on 19 July that year. These joined the AEC Regent Vs at Walsall under WMPTE, but had relatively short lives. *T. W. Moore*

Left and below: Walsall was allocated Guys during World War 2, while West Bromwich received Daimlers, but substandard austerity bodywork was common to them all. Operators' solutions to the premature deterioration of the bodies varied, but, apart from selling them early, options were to rebuild them extensively, transfer sound prewar bodies from worn-out chassis, or fit new bodies. Walsall and West Bromwich pursued all these options. Walsall 214 (JDH 36), combining a 1943 Guy Arab II chassis with a 1953 Willowbrook body, is seen leaving the town's St Paul's bus station in May 1965. West Bromwich 124 (BEA 724) was a 1945 Daimler CWA6 which received the Weymann body from a 1937 Daimler COG5 in 1958, but the replacement body has itself been substantially rebuilt. *(both) T. W. Moore*

Right: West Bromwich Corporation had need for just a few single-deckers. Despite its love of Daimlers, it eschewed that manufacturer's rather exotic Freeline model during the underfloor-engined era, and bought Leyland Tiger Cubs instead. The first three, built in 1958, were far from orthodox, however, because their 39-seat bodies were built by Mulliner, and featured rear entrances. No 213 is seen in Spon Lane in June 1965. All West Bromwich's Tiger Cubs were 7ft 6in-wide PSUC1/4 models with Pneumocyclic gearboxes.
Chris Aston

Far right: Time has surely not changed the view that the BMMO D9 is one of the sleekest half-cab double-deckers ever designed. Here 4949 loads at Walsall's St Paul's bus station on service 118, by then a joint service. The 1961 Metro-Cammell-bodied AEC Regent V alongside appears to be Walsall Corporation 893, but the date is August 1971 and the bus has been WMPTE 893L for nearly two years. *Malcolm Keeley*

Right: Harper Bros of Heath Hayes had its origins in the 1920s, and was the largest independent operator in the West Midland Traffic Area at the time of its takeover by Midland Red in 1974. Long lives were extracted from most of its buses. Leyland Royal Tiger PSU1/11 50 (XRE 725) of 1952 was bought new with Burlingham Seagull coachwork, but all the legendary elegance of that design was lost when the vehicle was rebuilt in 1967 with front entrance for bus work. It pauses near Heath Hayes on 8 April 1974. *Malcolm Keeley*

Right: Austin's of Woodseaves had a route network stretching from Bridgnorth to Cannock, and a fleet of around 50 vehicles in early postwar years. Rebuilds of older vehicles were a solution for small operators at that time of vehicle shortage. No 68 (RRF 308) had a 1949 registration and Harrington 33-seat coach body, but its Leyland Tiger TS4 chassis was actually new in 1932 as Oldham Corporation's BU 7102. A new body on such an old Leyland chassis was fairly unusual; the original petrol engine had been replaced by a Leyland 8.6-litre diesel. It is seen in Stafford in August 1960, the year before it was withdrawn.
Richard Butler

Below: The bus stance at Pitcher Bank, Stafford, displays an unusually strong Daimler emphasis in August 1951. OEH 294-300 were COG5/40 models built for Southern Rhodesia but, due to wartime shortages, were delivered to Potteries Motor Traction in 1942. The Weymann 39-seat bodies were 30ft long and 8ft wide — at that time longer and wider than normally allowed in the UK. They were originally registered HVT 816-22 but, unusually, received new marks upon rebuilding in 1950/1; they operated until 1959. The double-decker on the left is ex-Birmingham City Transport 1937 COG5/ Metro-Cammell COH 941, one of many with a variety of bodywork operated by Austin's of Woodseaves. *R. T. Wilson, courtesy BaMMOT*

Below: L418 (SRE 563), working PMT's Hanley–Stafford service, was one of three Crossley-bodied Crossleys acquired with the business of Mainwaring Bros, Bignall End, in June 1951. It was a DD42/7 model new in 1949. All three were re-engined with Leyland units in 1957 and ran for PMT until 1960. Note the PMT radiator badge. *Alan D. Broughall*

Left: Big queues in Station Street, Birmingham, as 1936 SON 1878 loads up on service 112 to Burton. Station Street was substantially shortened in the rebuilding of the Bull Ring area in the early 1960s. *G. H. Stone*

Gone for a Burton

The route to Burton-upon-Trent was the 112 or its onward extension, the X12 to Derby. Looking back through timetable books reflects the rise and fall in numbers travelling by bus. The 112 was increased from hourly to half-hourly in 1949, at last benefiting as Midland Red gathered enough vehicles to meet the growing demand in the early postwar years. The X12 extensions ran three times a day. Birmingham to Burton took 100 minutes and Derby a further 35. I suppose the running-time was not exceptionally slow, but, at least in my time, the A38 north of Lichfield had become a long, straight dual carriageway, and, as the old saying goes, it is a long road that has no turning, especially when the scenery is not exceptional.

Couple this with the disagreeable suspension of a BMMO S14, and you may gather that riding Midland Red could sometimes be a bit of an endurance!

The 112, however, did pass the company's Lichfield garage to the north of the city. This modern garage, opened in 1954, was a relatively small structure set within a much larger site. Judging by the amount of office accommodation and land, one imagines that Midland Red had expected the postwar increase in ridership to continue, but this was not to be, and instead the surplus land became the last resting-place of the company's vehicles before sale, generally for scrap. Travelling the territory meant one saw the new arrivals, but Lichfield was an essential stop to see what was disappearing as a consequence and to pay a final tribute to the battle-scarred veterans. My earliest visits saw the last survivors from the prewar fleet as, one

Right: Of the 100 LS18-class Leyland PSU3/4R Leopards delivered in 1962/3, half were originally to be bodied by Weymann. In the event only 25, including 5146 of Nuneaton garage, were so bodied and were clearly recognisable from their Willowbrook compatriots by the pleasantly curved roof profile above the destination boxes. BMMO badges featured on the front panels of all the LS18s (and the DD11 and DD12 Fleetlines) — an embellishment for which space was never found on any genuine BMMO single-deckers. No 5146 waits at Lichfield in 1964 with a well-laden BMMO S14 behind.
Tennent's Trains, Halesowen

34

Above: Whieldon's Green Bus commenced in 1927, and developed an important network in the Uttoxeter/ Cannock/ Lichfield triangle. The company liked Fodens, always rare but especially so prewar. Some were equipped with a weird choice of bodies, including No 40 (URF 873) which entered service in January 1951 with this King & Taylor 38-seat bus body. It ran until September 1967 and then had a short period as a towing vehicle. Green Bus also liked Guys, such as the ex-Southampton Arab seen behind in the earlier, more attractive livery superseded shortly before this March 1966 view at the Uttoxeter garage. Green Bus would sometimes buy large batches of secondhand vehicles, for example eventually operating 10 of these DTR-registered Park Royal-bodied Arabs. The company had no connection with Graham Martin's Warstone Motors, also known as Green Bus, which was founded in 1974 and operates in the same area as did Whieldon's. *Malcolm Keeley*

Above: A temporary central Birmingham terminus on what became St Martin's Ringway (later Queensway) for Lichfield's new S15 5051 in July 1962. The shell of the old Market Hall stands behind, the site soon to be cleared and excavated to create Manzoni Gardens, itself swept away in 2000 to make way for another redevelopment of the Bull Ring area.
Malcolm Keeley collection

by one, they were displaced from their later roles in the departmental fleet as tree-cutters, trainers etc. As each one went, I wondered if any souls would ever be brave enough to preserve an SOS, with, not least, their implications for spare parts; fortunately, they did. Longer-term residents were a few coach bodies retained for spares when their C2 and C3 chassis were rebodied by Plaxton around 1962 to modernise the tour fleet. All around would be evidence that the early postwar fleet that had engaged my interest was quickly disappearing. Finally, in 1965, the first of my precious 1953 LD8s appeared in the field, and it was clear that Midland Red was making little effort at selling them as runners. Leyland-bodied Leylands were capable of long lives: Birmingham City Transport did not make inroads into its 1949 batch until late 1967, by which time all the LD8s had gone. Nevertheless, I could understand that, especially at a time of staff shortages, bigger buses were more economical than a greater number of smaller ones, and that it was cheaper to replace rather than repair. Operators such as Ribble deliberately kept a modern profile and would sell buses after 12-13 years, but nobody sold Leyland-bodied Leylands for scrap at such an age, however hard they may have been worked. For the first time, I seriously began to wonder whether the company was losing its way.

Midland Red may have scrapped buses at 12 years of age, but things were quite different in Burton-upon-Trent. The brewery town's Corporation buses were wilfully old-fashioned, taking the desire for standardisation to extremes as technology left Burton

behind. The latest Daimlers continued to specify five-cylinder Gardner engines, Guy constant-mesh gearboxes and 12V electrical systems. All the older buses were Guys, which encouraged the view that most of the fleet comprised wartime austerity buses, although many of them were actually early postwar but, shall we say, conservative in appearance. Revolution came in 1969 with Daimler Fleetline single-deckers, followed subsequently by double-deck versions. New manager Roy Marshall breathed more life into the undertaking with a bright livery and new vehicles (assisted by shrewd secondhand purchases) to modernise operations.

Local authority reorganisation caused re-titling of the fleet in April 1974 as East Staffordshire District Council, which somehow sounded less impressive. Modernisation continued, particularly with Dennis Dominators, but uncertainty over the future saw operations taken over by Stevenson's in October 1985. Stevenson's, in turn, became joined to Midland Red North, the separate livery of which was washed away by Arriva corporate colours, bringing to an end the distinctive bus flavour enjoyed in Burton.

Back in the 1960s, Stevensons was a well-known (although not particularly large) independent, sitting in the vacuum between the three territorial operators, Midland Red, Potteries (PMT) and Trent. The fleet was mostly secondhand — no doubt an economic necessity of life in the largely-rural territory that provided its income until the East Staffs takeover, but the delight of Stevenson's was its apparent inability to buy two identical buses. Although Leylands tended to be in the majority, they were sourced from a variety of original operators and carried a wide selection from the catalogue of British bodybuilders.

The X12 would take us on to Derby. The Corporation there also had its own bus fleet, favouring Daimlers, but the tramways had been swept away by trolleybuses between 1930 and 1934. The last trolleybuses — eight Sunbeams — were delivered in 1960, but the following decade saw the replacement by motorbuses of the trolleybus system, which closed on 9 September 1967. A feature of postwar bus operations was the joint-working arrangement with Trent, including beyond the municipal boundaries. The most notable enterprise beyond the boundaries, however, began in 1973, when the much-admired independent Tailby & George (trading as Blue Bus Services) of Willington was taken over. Sadly the Willington garage was destroyed by fire in January 1976, this tragedy engulfing most of the ex-Blue Bus fleet. Derby's municipal buses joined the private sector in 1989.

Trent Motor Traction was a sister company in the BET group with Midland Red, and had its head office in Derby. The links with Midland Red included standardising on SOS vehicles in the late

Left: Three 1965 S17 shells were fitted out as prototypes for a new dual-purpose fleet. Nos 5722-4 were originally designated S21A, and each had a different interior to gauge passenger opinion; all three looked very attractive with black roofs. They eventually became classed as S17 buses and were withdrawn in 1977. This dismal spot for 5722 in March 1966 was New Street Park, the Burton terminus of service 112 — a long walk from Wetmore Park, the main centre for out-of-town buses working into Burton. *Maurice Collignon*

1920s and early 1930s. Late-1930s buses were more mixed, including AECs and Daimlers, but also some SOS saloons until war brought production to an end. All prewar double-deckers had forward entrances, another feature shared with Midland Red.

The early postwar years saw large orders placed for AECs, mostly with Willowbrook bodies, and many prewar buses were rebodied. A complete change of vehicle policy occurred in 1951 with a switch to Leylands. However, variety was once again evident in the 1960s, when AECs and Bedfords featured in the coach fleet; in the double-deck line, Daimler Fleetlines were preferred to Leyland's Atlantean from 1963. Trent passed to the National Bus Company and was greatly enlarged in early 1972 during the rationalisation of NBC subsidiary companies. Midland General was put under the company's wing, whilst the Buxton and Matlock garages and vehicles of North Western were added when that company was dismantled. NBC control brought the inevitable Leyland Nationals and Bristols, but Trent was one of the first to return to private hands, being bought by its management in December 1986.

One of the first acts of my long-time friend Tony Hall was to show me (in 1965) how to get all the way from Birmingham to Derby and then on to Nottingham by independent bus — the antidote to both the X12 and X99 (see next chapter)! Harper's legendary Leyland PD2 SBF 233 on its then-new service from central Birmingham to Cannock provided the vital first part of this exercise. The next bit required pre-planning, as the Green Bus of Rugeley link to that town was less frequent, but a lightweight coach met our need. At Rugeley we changed to one of Green Bus's ex-Southampton Guy double-deckers, this taking us to Uttoxeter, where Stevensons' ex-London Transport RTW (now preserved in Stevensons' colours) was ready for the next stage to Burton. One of Blue Bus's sublime Daimler CD650 double-deckers transported us to Derby, whence Barton could readily transport us to Nottingham. Our chosen route was the express to Nottingham, operated jointly by Barton and Trent. Barton's contribution was normally its low, low Loline, but the joint-running deal meant that on certain Saturdays Barton provided a second double-decker. On this occasion, Barton turned out No 734, the first of many Leyland Tiger PS1s rebodied as double-deckers, which made unforgettable and deafening progress along the fast road.

Left: The Burton fleet began to change radically from 1970. Four Leyland single-deckers — two Royal Tigers and two Tiger Cubs — were purchased secondhand from Bournemouth. No 1 was a 1954 Royal Tiger PSU1/13 with Burlingham bodywork, seen in March 1972. *Chris Aston*

Far left: Stevenson's of Spath, Uttoxeter, bought an assortment of ex-Sheffield buses in the early 1970s including, in 1971, 3908/14 WE, the two 1958 Leyland Titan PD3/1s with Roe 73-seat bodies seen here in May 1974 at the then Burton garage. Stevenson's fitted the pair with platform doors but, judging by the thrashing but slow ride of the one I travelled upon, initially did nothing about the rear-axle ratio, which remained resolutely suited to Sheffield's hills rather than the open roads of semi-rural Staffordshire. *Malcolm Keeley*

Left: Enthusiasts' favourites in a fleet that was an enthusiasts' favourite were the four rare Daimler CD650 buses of Blue Bus Services of Willington. These had powerful Daimler 10.6-litre engines and preselector gearboxes which gave a smooth, mellow ride, whilst the Willowbrook bodies, although unfortunately 'lowbridge' (side gangway upstairs) due to the territory, were sumptuously appointed. SRB 424, new in 1953, passes through Findern in March 1968. *Martin Llewellyn*

Right: There was always a lot more going on at Wetmore Park bus station in Burton. Midland Red 1933 IM4 1461 (HA 8356) dominates this view taken around 1950, the year when the bus was withdrawn. It belongs to the last batch of IM family buses, which had bodies by Short Bros to a more modern design; the radiused windows, with half-drop ventilators, foreshadowed the ON models introduced the following year. *Roy Marshall*

Far right: Half a decade on and 1949 BMMO S9 3361 occupies the same spot with new D7 4410 loading behind. *Peter Yeomans*

Right: Stevenson's was another operator to have begun in the mid-1920s. Its main services ran between Uttoxeter and Burton-upon-Trent (Wetmore Park). I know it winds up London Transport fans, but the frequently odd vehicle-selling policies of the Capital's bus operator were a great help to undercapitalised independents, like Stevenson's, with thin territories. KGK 724, a 1949 RT-class AEC Regent with Cravens bodywork, was one of a youthful pair bought in 1957, and ran until 1972. The arrival in the Stevenson's fleet of four ex-Burton Guy Arab IIIs, including 1946 Brush-bodied 28 (FA 8420), as early as 1954 does not seem due to LT, but was achieved as a result of Burton's replacing single-deckers prematurely by acquiring six ex-London Guy double-deckers. Despite their austerity specification, the London Guys ran in Burton until the mid-1960s, and one, HGC 130, survives in preservation to represent London's Guys. *Alan D. Broughall*

Far left: Many of Burton's Guys looked like wartime austerity buses even when they were not. The gloomy maroon livery did not help. This Gardner 5LW-powered Guy Arab III with 53-seat lowbridge Roberts bodywork, numbered 4 (FA 8597) and pictured in April 1960, actually dated from 1947 and was one of six. *Richard Butler*

Left: Derby Corporation standardised on Brush-bodied Daimler COG5 models in the late 1930s, and received more Daimlers during World War 2. The problem of substandard wartime bodywork was resolved on 1944 CWA6 7 (RC 8427) by fitting the 1938 body from a COG5. It waits for work near Corporation Street in August 1959. *Richard Butler*

Left: One does not associate a 'quality' operator such as Trent with the need to push-start buses, but 1946 AEC Regent II/Willowbrook 1118 (RC 8916) needed a helping hand at Derby bus station in April 1960. Although the body was quite different, the chassis was very similar to Midland Red's AD2 class. *Richard Butler*

Right: Derby 179 (RC 8879) was one of 10 Sunbeam W trolleybuses delivered in 1946 with Park Royal bodies that still carried the appearance of wartime austerity vehicles. It is seen on London Road in August 1963 and ran until 1965. *Martin Llewellyn*

Far right: After years of Daimler motorbuses, Derby Corporation received some extraordinary purchases in 1952. They were five Foden PVD6 and five Crossley buses, in both cases amongst the last to be built. The Crossleys were of the rare DD42/8A model. To cap it all, they were bodied by Brush, which ceased building bus bodies immediately afterwards. No 107 (CRC 907) was one of the Fodens, and is seen at work on Siddals Road in May 1965. *Chris Aston*

Gone for a Barton

If the 112/X12 to Burton involved a depressing ride along the A38, then the X99 from Birmingham to Nottingham called for a Samaritan, instead of a conductor, to counsel the passengers. This was a desperately slow route, despite its glamorous 'X' prefix (which the innocent might have thought implied limited stops), and could test the friendship of any couple, let alone two early-teenage boys. The only way to make the journey tolerable was to undertake it in portions. There were lots of Midland Red buses as far as Sutton Coldfield, while service 110 provided fitted timings with X99 to give a good frequency to Tamworth; both towns had Midland Red garages.

It was ironic that Sutton Coldfield enjoyed the reputation of being 'posh', despite the odd rough estate carefully hidden away, as the buses belonging to the Midland Red garage in the town were amongst the shabbiest in the fleet! For many years the garage held a special surprise, however, because it also housed the bus owned by the Sutton Coldfield Old People's Welfare Committee. This was a rare AEC Q, CGJ 188, wearing an orange and cream livery applied

in a manner that would be considered eccentric even today. Happily this exceptional survivor passed into preservation.

As mentioned in the Introduction, the prime purpose of my first X99 exploration was to see Barton Transport, and its buses first became prominent at Long Eaton. The approach to Nottingham included Beeston, the company's base. Ironically, Barton itself used to run to Birmingham, but in 1932 exchanged its work for the Leicester–Nottingham service that became Barton route 12. No operator today can match the glories of Barton, which remained independent when most large bus undertakings were either local authorities or owned by one of the two big groups: BET and the nationalised British Transport Commission. Barton bought small batches of buses and coaches new, often with distinctive styling or trim, but augmented these with significant numbers of secondhand vehicles, no doubt to ensure modern, high-depreciation vehicles did not sit idly around garages between peaks. Many old buses, usually Leylands, were extensively rebuilt or rebodied. Leyland was, for many years, the preferred make, but, I was told, the manufacturer fell out with Barton, which labelled rebuilds as Barton rather than Leyland products. AEC buses and coaches thus became the general choice for new stock in the late 1950s and throughout the 1960s, but

Right: No 1153 (HA 6158) dated from 1930 and was a Short Bros-bodied IM4. It loads at Ashby-de-la-Zouch on service 699 to Moira and Overseal in October 1949, the year it was withdrawn. *D. F. Tee*

Left: Very different ideas on producing dual-purpose vehicles at Mount Street bus station, Nottingham, in May 1958. Midland Red BMMO S15 4604 of Coalville garage, loading for Birmingham on service X99, was new the previous year. Trent's approach to creating 20 dual-purpose models in 1958 was to take 1947 AEC Regal 35-seat buses, extend the Willowbrook bodies to 30ft, modernise with full-width cabs and fit 39 superior seats. No 300 (RC 9663) was the first and also featured new flush glazed windows. *Richard Butler*

they were forever accompanied by an army of secondhand Leylands, which gave the impression that the company's heart remained with the Lancashire builder. All changed in the mid-1970s, when the existing fleet was swept away by Bus Grant-specification Leyland and Bedford coaches, removing seemingly overnight the fleet's interest, although I imagine most travellers would have considered the new régime an improvement. Barton sold out to long-time rival Trent, as prominent in Nottingham as in Derby, in the summer of 1989.

Three fleets in the North Midlands were owned for many years by the Midland Counties Electric Supply Co, which was part of the Balfour Beatty Group. The three, Mansfield District, Midland General and Notts & Derby, passed to the British Transport Commission in 1948, when the electricity-supply industry was nationalised. Their route into the BTC was thus different from that of most BTC companies, which were generally 'voluntary' sales and largely ex-Tilling Group. Despite the enforced introduction of Bristol vehicles, they retained a distinctive air, particularly the two prominent in Nottingham, Midland General and Notts & Derby, whose immaculate buses were painted blue and cream in distinctly non-Tilling proportions.

Notts & Derby was the senior of the two companies, having operated trams, which were replaced by trolleybuses in 1931-3. Midland General had been set up in 1920 as a bus-operating subsidiary, and by the end of the decade had outgrown its parent. The trolleybuses were withdrawn in 1953, but the Notts & Derby name was retained on the bus replacements. The National Bus Company inherited the BTC companies, and, as 1971 moved into 1972, Notts & Derby's vehicles and routes passed to Midland General, which became managed by Trent from the same date. The Midland General name was retained by Trent for several years, but all vehicles became NBC poppy red.

Notts & Derby was a rare example of company trolleybus operation. The trolleybus was essentially an urban beast, and, as such, was most associated with municipal operators. Nottingham City Transport introduced trolleybuses in 1927, being sufficiently enthused to replace all its trams with them by 1936. AEC was the favourite for the City Transport motorbus fleet, although other makes, such as Daimler and, later, Leyland, crept in. In the early 1960s, NCT possessed an interesting, solid-looking fleet of buses and trolleybuses but no particular claim to fame. The trolleybuses were replaced by motorbuses between 1962 and 1966, during which time the livery was updated and the body design of the replacing Daimler, Leyland and AEC vehicles grew increasingly idiosyncratic as the operator sought interchangeability of regularly-damaged parts despite employing a variety of builders. Soon Nottingham had its own distinctive style, which seemed appropriate when, after so many

Right: Twenty of the 100 LS18-class Leyland Leopards delivered to Midland Red in 1962/3 were finished to dual-purpose specification, reducing the seating capacity from 53 to 48. They looked fine with black roofs and a little polished trim. Tamworth's 5190, with Willowbrook body, loads in Mount Street bus station, Nottingham, in June 1966. *Malcolm Keeley Collection*

Far right: It is not hard to imagine the exhaust reverberating off the walls as LS20-class Leyland Leopard 5845 powers out of Nottingham back to Birmingham on 20 July 1972. This class of PSU3/4R models was only 10-strong and entered service in 1967. The Willowbrook 49-seat dual-purpose bodies originally had black roofs and more brightwork, but successive unsympathetic repaints gradually reduced their fine appearance. The lettering is of the style, edged in black, favoured from October 1970 until imposition of National Bus Company corporate livery from late summer 1972. In this case the lettering is in silver to denote dual-purpose bus/coach status; most buses would have received yellow. *Richard Butler*

Right: Nottingham 109 is a delightful example of an early postwar municipal bus. A 1949 AEC Regent III with preselective gearbox and 56-seat body by Metro-Cammell, it was one of 30 of this combination received by the Corporation. It is seen in West Bridgford amidst encroaching urban development at the Greythorn Drive terminus of the joint Nottingham/West Bridgford service 15 on 28 May 1960. *Richard Butler*

Right: 4 May 1959 was a special day in Nottingham. The city was brought to a standstill when Nottingham Forest football team toured the centre with the FA Cup won the previous Saturday. The ensuing congestion exacerbated the bus queues leading to superb atmospheric transport scenes, such as this view in Trinity Square. Nottingham City Transport purchased 65 of these handsome Park Royal-bodied AEC Regent Vs in 1955/6, which took the numbers 209-73. Behind, new Leyland Titan PD2/ Metro-Cammell No 33 awaits its next duty. Since World War 2, Nottingham had become one of those neat fleets that liked matching fleet and registration numbers. *Richard Butler*

Far right: Barton bought many secondhand buses in the early postwar years. No 584 was a 1939 Leyland TD5 with a Roe body, one of a number of assorted Leylands originating with West Riding purchased in 1949/50. This source of good vehicles dried up when West Riding took over the operations of Bullock, Featherstone, in 1950, and the replacement of ex-Bullock buses became West Riding's priority for the next few years. This delightful view shows 584 singing its way through countryside near Owthorpe, *en route* to Nottingham on 2 May 1959. It ran until April 1960, so it owed Barton nothing. *Richard Butler*

of the big-city fleets were swallowed up into PTEs, NCT became the biggest municipal bus fleet in England.

Joint services, commencing in 1928 between Nottingham City Transport and West Bridgford Urban District Council, brought the latter's own bus fleet, again largely AEC since the 1930s, into central Nottingham. A new postwar housing estate at Clifton became a *cause célèbre* in the traffic courts in those pre-deregulation days due to its geographical location and access via a route outside the city boundary and over another operator's service. The upshot was a joint service by Nottingham, West Bridgford UDC and the independent South Notts. Lowbridge buses were required, and in the early days NCT and the UDC both used secondhand utility Daimlers, from Bradford and

Huddersfield respectively, although the UDC also took a saw to a prewar Regent and converted it to lowbridge. Nottingham took over the West Bridgford fleet in 1968, but South Notts lasted until after deregulation, finally succumbing to the big operator in 1991.

Needless to say, all these operators and more did not fit into one bus station. The enthusiast visitor had to learn the way between Mount Street, Broad Marsh and Huntingdon Street bus stations, as well as significant on-street termini such as Old Market Square and King Street. How lucky we are that Nottingham has generated some of the country's best bus photographers, the most senior being Geoffrey Atkins, who undoubtedly showed those that followed how it should be done.

Right: West Bridgford Urban District Council Passenger Transport Department was one of the smallest municipal fleets in the country despite having one of the longest names. This ended on 28 September 1968 when its buses were taken over by Nottingham City Transport. Good maintenance led to long lives, and this 1947 AEC Regent III with Park Royal body survived long enough to be transferred. No 3 (HNN 773) loads in Old Market Square, Nottingham, in May 1965. The unmistakable service numbers on these buses were 19in high. *Martin Llewellyn*

Far right: Typical of Barton's delicious vehicles was No 262, seen in Huntingdon Street bus station, Nottingham, on 6 June 1960, surrounded by contract buses of Greyhound of Sheffield. It was a Leyland Lion LT7, new in 1936 with Duple dual-purpose bus/coach body. World War 2 saw it rebodied with a Burlingham 'utility' bus body in 1944, but five years later it received a new Duple coach body as carried here — a relatively straightforward history compared to some of the same batch which got involved in more complex chassis/body swaps! The compact design of the LT7 allowed 39 seats in the Duple bodies. *Richard Butler*

51

Right: W. Gash & Sons of Newark bought a tasty fleet of nine Daimler CVD6 double-deckers in 1948-50, principally for its main-road route to Nottingham. The first four had Strachans bodies, which were replaced by Massey between 1958 and 1962, and went on to achieve very long lives. DD4 (KNN 622) is seen at Huntingdon Street bus station, Nottingham, in September 1958, still with its original Strachans body. Hall Bros was a coach operator based in South Shields with services between the eastern Midlands and northeast England; it was acquired by Barton in 1967. *Richard Butler*

Right: The large Clifton estate brought the need for lowbridge buses into the West Bridgford fleet, including three 1958 AEC Regent Vs with rare Reading 59-seat bodies. No 31 (XVO 329) makes a splash through floodwater in Clifton Lane, Wilford, on 31 January 1960. *Richard Butler*

Far left: The Notts & Derby trolleybus system was replaced by motorbuses in April 1953. The closing fleet comprised 17 AEC 661T trolleybuses built between 1937 and 1942 and 15 BUT 9611T vehicles dating from 1949, all with Weymann 56-seat bodies. All 32 passed to Bradford City Transport for further service. No 300 (DRB 616) was numerically the oldest in the fleet. *S. E. Letts*

Left: Representing East Midland at Huntingdon Street bus station, Nottingham, in September 1958 was D8 (BAL 708), one of 12 1935/6 Leyland TD4 Titans rebodied by Willowbrook in 1949 and retained by East Midland until 1959/60. *Richard Butler*

Left: Construction of Clifton Estate meant double-deckers were introduced to the South Notts fleet. Both new and secondhand Leylands were acquired, all with low-height bodies. Amongst the secondhand acquisitions was 66 (HNU 815), an ex-Chesterfield TD5 with Weymann body, seen at Huntingdon Street bus station in July 1958. *Richard Butler*

Right: South Notts bought two of these 1951 Leyland Royal Tiger PSU1/15s from Jackson of Castle Bromwich in 1957. The bodies are of the Duple Roadmaster style immortalised as a Dinky Toy, which was rather more numerous than the real thing. No 64 (LOE 300) heads three South Notts buses at Huntingdon Street bus station in April 1966; 1951 all-Leyland PD2/12 48 and 1962 Northern Counties-bodied Leyland PD3/4 80 stand behind. *Malcolm Keeley*

Far right: Very much Trent's equivalent to Midland Red's D7 was the Leyland Titan PD2/12 with Metro-Cammell Orion lightweight body, of which 50 were received in 1956/7. The sun casts long shadows as No 773 (KCH 116) leaves Nottingham in July 1965. *Martin Llewellyn*

Inset right: Weymann-bodied AEC Regent III JVO 949 got about a bit within the three Balfour Beatty companies that passed to the British Transport Commission. It was new in 1948 to Mansfield District, but was one of 12 transferred as part of the trolleybus-replacement fleet to Notts & Derby in 1953, receiving fleetnumber 323. In 1965 Notts & Derby received a considerable number of large-capacity Bristol FLFs, which made many of the Regents redundant. They still had life left in them, however, so they passed to Midland General for their last year or two of service. No 323 looks very tidy at Mount Street, Nottingham, on 19 March 1966. *Malcolm Keeley*

Lingering in Leicestershire

Leicester was a major centre of operation for Midland Red, requiring three substantial company garages accommodating around 200 vehicles, not including nearby premises at Coalville and Markfield. Midland Red had fought a mighty campaign against small companies around Leicester in the 1920s, including the incident of the 22-stone bus inspector who 'accidentally' leant on an opposition driver with his arm across the latter's windpipe while the Midland Red bus loaded and got away first from the terminus. Then, in the decade after the regulation created by the Road Traffic Act, 1930, the company acquired the interests of around 60 operators in Leicestershire, plus the bus services of many more which turned to coach and private-hire operations. Additionally, the impressive Leicester City Transport was prominent in the city, and a number of notable independents survived.

The principal route to Leicester from Birmingham was the X68 via Coventry, operated by standard double-deckers taking just over two hours from end to end. At the height of the postwar travel boom the X68 ran hourly, increased to half-hourly on Saturdays.

The X68, together with its X69 short working to Coventry, was also a regular means for Leicester enthusiasts to gain access to other parts of the Midland Red system. Those wishing to maximise the value of their 'Day Anywhere' ticket could make a departure from Leicester as early as 0525. Birmingham Digbeth garage had one bus on this otherwise Leicester-worked route, so the more restrained enthusiast would favour the 0910 departure which gave Leicester enthusiasts a rare chance to sample LD8-class Leylands, which were not allocated to the city until odd examples went there at the end of their lives. Leicester's own transport department had lots of Leylands, of course, but Midland Red's LD8s had a sound and character unique to themselves. Midland Red's 1950s takeovers of Kemp & Shaw and Boyer brought two Leyland Titans and a Leyland Royal Tiger into the fleet. Strangely these remained at Leicester, though they would have fitted in better at Leyland-inclined garages such as Leamington and Ludlow.

Not that Midland Red's Leicester allocation was otherwise entirely BMMO. The same takeovers also brought in Gardner-engined Guys, previously familiar in the city with the company's own allocation of austerity Guys, and having rather less in common with the GD6 Guys at Dudley with BMMO engines replacing their original Meadows units. The two ex-Boyer Sentinels would have found difficulty fitting in anywhere in the country, let alone Midland Red. The company's early postwar AD2 class of AEC Regent IIs with 7.7-litre engines, burdened by rather heavy bodies, were found in numbers in the city, which had relatively undemanding geography.

Heaven forbid that the writer should give the impression that Birmingham is the centre of the universe, because Midland Red's Leicester network could boast a selection of other useful if infrequent 'X' services to destinations such as Northampton, Rugby, Shrewsbury and, for a time, Derby. Leicester, unlike Birmingham, even enjoyed a link twice a day to Hereford with the X91 via Coventry, Stratford and Worcester. This marathon took 5½ hours each way and gave the Leicester traveller only 95 minutes in Hereford before returning, so he or she needed to be keen. Even the crews didn't make it all the way, the route being timed so the vehicles crossed at Stratford-upon-Avon, where the crews exchanged and returned home. Finally there was the X60 to Corby and Weldon, operated on Wednesdays and Sundays, which, on Saturdays, was operated by United Counties as its service 264. A contemporary Midland Red *Staff Bulletin* records that, on 2 October 1965, Mr R. Lacey of Leicester covered 355.66 miles on his 'Day Anywhere' ticket, using routes L7, X69, 658, X97, X35, X91, 725 and 658 again. His record was subsequently beaten, but only by repeated use of the Birmingham–Worcester motorway service!

The Leicester timetable handily included details of operators such as Barton, Gibson Bros, Howlett of Quorn, Hylton & Dawson and Trent, as well as a list of Leicester City Transport services. An operator would, in the first instance, attract me if it ran double-deckers, but, secondly, it needed to terminate in the same place as

Right: This prewar X68 Birmingham–Leicester departure, seen at Wolvey, gets the benefit of an unidentified member of the 1934/5 LRR class; these coaches would be relegated to bus use in 1940/1. The driver and conductor wear quite different uniforms, being ultimately under the separate controls of Mr Shire, Chief Engineer, and Mr Power, Traffic Manager, respectively. *R. T. Wilson, courtesy BaMMOT*

Left: Digbeth-allocated D7 4509 approaches Allesley, Coventry, in October 1967, making slow progress along the wrong side of the A45 dual carriageway following a traffic accident. *T. W. Moore*

Midland Red for me to know about them. Firms running into St Margaret's bus station, such as Astill & Jordan and Brown's Blue, therefore instantly engaged my interest, whilst gems such as the Crossleys of Gibson were relatively hidden away in Western Boulevard.

Leicester City Transport had decided to scrap its tram system in 1938, and initially favoured three-axle AEC Renowns as replacements. World War 2 intervened, but between 1948 and 1950 there was an immense vehicle intake, comprising Leyland, AEC and Daimler double-deckers, which replaced the last tramcars (in November 1949) and most prewar buses too. Fleet renewal recommenced in earnest from 1958, and the period until 1969 was largely Leyland, originally with Titan PD3s but eventually Atlanteans. There followed a period of interest in single-deckers, with Bristol REs from 1967 to 1970 and Metro-Scanias in 1971/2. Double-deckers returned to favour in 1974 but, until Dennis came up with the Dominator, the Anglo-Swedish combination ruled. I remember the general manager singing the praises of his Scanias

over the previous Leylands. I guess he wasn't around to pick up the pieces when the legendary corrosion hit the Metro-Scanias although, unlike most other operators, Leicester did persevere with them. After the break-up of the old Midland Red, Leicester became the heartland of Midland Fox (now part of Arriva), which has given LCT and its privatised successors a good run.

Following our initial foray, Leicester became part of much longer, circular 'bashes'. The 658 route between Leicester, Hinckley, Nuneaton and Coventry, worked by and travelling via towns with Midland Red garages, became for us a more useful artery than the X68 and had an enviable frequency. If I had been a little less obsessed with vehicles, I could have travelled out as far as Grantham via Melton Mowbray on service 662. This was a joint service with Lincolnshire Road Car, the buses of which, rather confusingly, showed service 25. Needless to say, 'Day Anywhere' tickets were not valid on the Lincolnshire buses, diminishing the opportunities presented by the joint hourly headway. Perhaps I would have made the trip if I had known Barton had a major presence in Melton!

Far left: D9 5318, one of Hinckley garage's regular contributions to service 658, loads in April 1968 at a Pool Meadow bus station not yet overlooked by Coventry's inner ring road. The bus has the traditional transfers, while the side advertisement for the company's coach tours is of a style first used on publicity material, but extended to the buses themselves from the end of 1968 — initially on newer buses only and then all vehicles from June 1970. This ended a confused period of fleetname styles over the previous five years, but all was to be swept away by NBC corporate liveries from August 1972. *Malcolm Keeley*

Left: Examples of Midland Red's 100-strong AD2 class of AEC Regent II buses were a familiar sight around St Margaret's bus station, Leicester, for many years, including 3192, seen in March 1960. The order for bodies to BMMO design was split equally between Brush and Metro-Cammell, and it was not difficult to tell the two apart. Dividing the order was intended to speed deliveries of new double-deckers to the company; delivery began in 1948, but the 50 Metro-Cammell examples were so slow in arriving that many of BMMO's own D5 products were in service by the time they arrived. No 3192 was actually new to Black Country garage Oldbury in April 1950, but moved to Leicestershire's Hinckley garage as early as June 1951 and again to Leicester, Sandacre Street, in May 1952. *Peter G. Smith*

Right: The S16 was the first BMMO design of 36ft-long bus, introduced in 1962. It retained the 8-litre engine and crash gearbox of its shorter predecessors, so performance was not glittering; the S17 with 10.5-litre engine and semi-automatic gearbox soon superseded it. No 5104 works the X91 Leicester–Hereford service; the bus seating was not really adequate for such a long run but clearly those extra seats were needed. This photograph at Pool Meadow, Coventry, illustrates how the existing, relatively short window bays were continued into the S16/17 designs, exaggerating the greater length. No 5104 was then working from Leicester's Southgate Street garage, but would become one of the few S16s to pass to WMPTE in 1973. *Roy Marshall*

Right: Monty Moreton was one of several independents competing in Nuneaton with Midland Red in the 1920s, but by 1939 the big company had taken over all except Monty. The other well-known big independent in the town, Lloyd's, concentrated on excursions, private hires and factory services, rather than bus services. Purchased by Monty in 1964, 525 LMJ had been built the previous year as a Bedford demonstrator; it was a VAL14 with Duple (Midland) 53-seat bodywork. Midland Red S12 3745 lies in wait as the VAL circuits Nuneaton bus station. This was not the most exciting place in the world architecturally, but a good enough spot to enjoy BMMO sound effects. For a fee the writer will still impersonate the distinctive chuffing noise made by an early postwar S-type being hammered the length of Nuneaton bus station in first gear with engine on the governor.
T. W. Moore

Left: What it was all about . . . looking around a garage, hoping to find something really different! We remembered SON-class buses in service, and continued to find odd ones as departmental vehicles, but the discovery of HA 9481 at Leicester, Southgate Street, with its two-letter, four-numeral registration really made our day, just as survivors like HA 2250 and HA 2453 had turned the heads of an earlier generation. Perhaps it still happens today, but I suspect the preservation movement has taken the spirit of discovery out of it. HA 9481 had been formerly bus 1530, and was actually numerically the first of three DON-class prototypes built in 1934, all initially with AEC 7.7-litre engines — the company's first 'diesel' buses. It worked as a tree-cutter from 1951 to 1963. *Alan D. Broughall*

Left: An early advertisement for 'Day Anywhere' tickets in an April 1928 timetable book. Note that a prime market was commercial travellers, before company cars became universal.

Far left: The driver of 1951 BMMO D5B 3862 carefully picks his way amongst passengers walking to and from the bus bays at St Margaret's bus station, Leicester. This bus had a 15-year life. *Alan D. Broughall*

Far left: The crew has time for a smoke at the X68 terminus on the forecourt of Leicester's Southgate Street garage before removing the wheel-chock and returning 1953 LD8 Leyland PD2/12 4000 home to Birmingham in March 1960. No 4000 was one of several new to Oldbury, but, like the AD2s, they were soon moved on in favour of BMMO products. A D7 displaced 4000 to Digbeth in October 1956, the latter's interurban work being ideally suited to these buses. *Peter G. Smith*

Left: A comparison between 4000 and a standard Leyland-bodied Leyland PD2/12 is offered by this view of 4845, taken over from Kemp & Shaw. The 1952 bus is seen at St Margaret's bus station in May 1965, alongside D9 5010, delivered new to Leicester, Sandacre Street in October 1962. No 5010 remained at Leicester, moving briefly to Southgate Street a few months before its September 1974 withdrawal. *Martin Llewellyn*

Left: Midland Red built up a large fleet of Daimler Fleetlines with Alexander bodies. The first 50 arrived in 1963, and the penultimate example, 5293, is seen on Aylestone Road in May 1964 as an LS18-class Leyland Leopard passes in the opposite direction against a background of spring laburnum. One Fleetline, 5261, ran for some years with its original Gardner 6LX engine replaced by a 10.5-litre BMMO — certainly a unique combination. *Martin Llewellyn*

Page 65 lower left: Midland Red acquired the share capital of Kemp & Shaw on 31 July 1955, and ran the company as a subsidiary until 1 January 1959. The subsidiary operated routes from Leicester to Derby, Loughborough and Birstall (Windmill Avenue), the Derby route being passed to Trent in April 1961. One 1943 Guy was withdrawn in 1955, but the remainder of the fleet lasted long enough to receive Midland Red colours upon the 1959 absorption. Included were four Northern Counties-bodied Guy Arabs with Gardner 5LW engines. Kemp & Shaw 27 (EJF 669) was a 1948 Arab III, seen here at St Margaret's on 27 December 1958. It became Midland Red 4841 and ran until 1961.
Richard Butler

Right: Despite its many rural routes, Midland Red managed without side-gangway 'lowbridge' double-deckers, but Kemp & Shaw had one which subsequently ran until 1967 in the BMMO fleet. This was Kemp & Shaw 30 (GRY 763), a 1950 all-Leyland Titan PD2/1, seen here in August 1958 in the subsidiary's colours but already with BMMO destination layout and 'Kemp & Shaw' in the traditional illuminated box above.
Richard Butler

Left: Midland Red's retaining acquired vehicles was a rare event but, one month after the Kemp & Shaw absorption, on 1 February 1959, Boyer of Rothley was taken over, with three vehicles entering the fleet. Two were 1951 Sentinels which, as a Brummie, I only ever saw lounging around St Margaret's on my infrequent visits to Leicester. Confirmation that they did move is provided by this view of 4847 (GUT 543), an STC6/44 model with Sentinel's own 44-seat body, loading in Lemyngton Street, Loughborough, in January 1960. The pair were withdrawn in 1961/3. *Richard Butler*

Below: Boyer's durable 1952 Leyland Royal Tiger PSU1/9 with Leyland's own 44-seat bodywork, HJU 546, new to Allen of Mountsorrell, lasted until 1966 as Midland Red 4848, and moved on to a fourth owner, Stevenson's, for even more work. It is seen here in Garden Street, Leicester, on the last Saturday of Boyer operation, passing to Midland Red that night. This street was used for many years as an unloading point for all routes approaching St Margaret's bus station from the Belgrave Road/Belgrave Gate direction. *Peter G. Smith*

Below: No 3441 was one of Midland Red's more distinctive vehicles. One of 100 S9-class buses built with Brush bodies in 1949, its entry into service was delayed because it was the prototype for the new 'American'-style front end with power doors. It is believed, although not conclusively, that 3441 was delivered as standard from Brush and that the modifications were carried out at Carlyle Works. After experimental work, it entered passenger service at Leicester, Sandacre Street in October 1950, and remained there until withdrawal in 1963. It was typical of BMMO at that time to adorn a prototype liberally with brightwork, still much in evidence at St Margaret's bus station in August 1963. It was initially used to launch the new X97 to Shrewsbury, a service announced over previous weeks by a company loudspeaker van touring the route. *Chris Aston*

Above: Gibson Bros had around 16 vehicles, of which roughly half were for stage-carriage work. The most important services were between Leicester and Market Bosworth. A fleet of double-deckers was maintained, occasionally supplemented by coaches. This 1950 Strachans-bodied Crossley DD42/7, No 29 (FNR 597), seen at the Barlestone garage in May 1962, was one of a pair bought new. Strachans products were not particularly durable, and the 56-seat body had been heavily rebuilt by this time. *Peter G. Smith*

Left: Brown's Blue of Markfield was for years the largest independent operator in Leicestershire, running around 50 vehicles including a fleet of double-deckers supplemented by coaches on stage services. This sunny scene at the Ibstock depot, with driver at the wheel, conveys a bright future, but this is the day after the Midland Red takeover on 16 March 1963, and none of the vehicles was added to the new owner's fleet. Midland Red retained the Markfield depot for a few years, keeping around 15 vehicles there until its closure at the end of June 1968, the allocation passing to nearby Coalville. HTT 333 started life with Devon General and was one of the small batch of RT-type Regents built for provincial operators in 1946/7 prior to introduction of the more familiar style of Regent III with higher radiator and bonnet line. The body is by Weymann. *Chris Aston*

Right: Blockley of Heather, trading as Ruby Coaches, was primarily a coach operator but did run bus services. This 1932 Dennis Lancet I, modernised with an AEC 7.7-litre diesel engine and 1946 Yeates body, clad in the company's maroon and red colours, loads in Coalville on a wet August day in 1960. The registration, JU 1000, would be worth a fortune today. *Richard Butler*

Right: Leicester City Transport bought 20 Leyland PD1 buses with Leyland's own 56-seat bodies in 1946. Barton Transport purchased most of them when they were withdrawn in 1959/60, no doubt finding them still in excellent condition. As if to prove the point, former Leicester 248 stages a return to its erstwhile home city whilst working as Barton 834 on 6 June 1960. Midland Red BMMO S6 3047 looks on at St Margaret's bus station. *Richard Butler*

Left: Both Astill & Jordan and Hylton & Dawson operated between Leicester and Glenfield. The latter's small fleet was painted maroon, cream and blue. This 1946 AEC Regal/Harrington, ADO 513, was purchased from Camplin of Donnington, and only ran for around a year with Hylton & Dawson. It is seen with baggy-trousered conductor in St Margaret's bus station on 28 September 1956. *Richard Butler*

Far left: The blue- and cream-painted fleet of Astill & Jordan favoured double-deckers, assisted by coaches. MFD 643 was a 1952 rebuild of a 1935 AEC Regent chassis, new to Cardiff Corporation as KG 5005; lengthened to 30ft and rebodied by W. S. Yeates, it was initially operated in its new guise by Davenport of Netherton. Astill & Jordan owned it from December 1958 until January 1964. It is seen leaving St Margaret's bus station. *Alan D. Broughall*

Left: The 1951/2 Bristol LWL buses with ECW 39-seat bodies would be the last new half-cab single-deckers received by United Counties before it moved on to the underfloor-engined LS model. Steeped in the Tilling mindset that any bus displaying good performance must be wasting money, United Counties exchanged the original Bristol AVW 8.15-litre engines for Gardner 5LW 7-litre units in the mid-1950s. No 403 (CNH 847) is surrounded by Birmingham-bound BMMO D7s, including Digbeth's 4355, at Southgate Street, Leicester, on a Saturday in August 1960. *Richard Butler*

Right: No fewer than 65 preselector-gearbox AEC Regent III buses were introduced by Leicester City Transport in 1948. Of these, 31 were bodied by Metro-Cammell and the remainder Brush. No 44, with Brush bodywork, was fresh from repaint when approaching the Highway Road terminus of service 30 in July 1961. The blind has been reset for the return journey to Glenfield Road, but the number has not yet been altered to 16. These Brush bodies particularly interested me, because they were clearly related to those by the same builder for Birmingham City Transport — one supplied in 1946 as the postwar prototype and mounted on prewar Daimler COG5 1235, followed by 100 on Leyland Titan PD2 chassis in 1948/9 (1656-1755). *Peter G. Smith*

Far right: A brighter livery was introduced for newer buses in the Leicester fleet from May 1961. New Park Royal-bodied AEC Bridgemaster 220 waits in Humberstone Gate during September 1962, where the backdrop today would be the Haymarket Shopping Centre. Ladies from a tour coach file into the Bell Hotel, looking forward to their inclusive lunch. Leicester bought 10 Bridgemasters, delivery being spread over the years 1959 to 1962, but all were withdrawn in May 1971. The Transport Department developed a bad habit of cramming extra seats into its buses, for example somehow managing to squeeze 76 seated passengers into these Bridgemasters, with no fewer than 45 unfortunate victims being accommodated upstairs.
Peter G. Smith

71

Northampton and Across to Banbury

The legendary X96 Shrewsbury–Wolverhampton–Birmingham–Coventry–Northampton service, introduced in 1930 and one of the longest stage-carriage services in the UK, took over five hours from end to end. Using the X96 required a bit of planning and left no room for slip-ups because, in our 'Day Anywhere' days, it ran only every four hours.

The X96 was clearly regarded by Midland Red as special, and had the distinction of being the only *bus* route to go into Birmingham's Digbeth *coach* station. Its minimum-fare, limited-stop status between Wolverhampton and Coventry also gave the X96 an exclusivity, leaving lesser mortals behind for other services to pick up.

Travelling east from Birmingham, the next significant area of transport interest was Coventry. One of the passenger transport industry's most respected general managers was appointed to Coventry Corporation Transport in 1933. Mr R. A. Fearnley soon laid

his stamp on the bus and tram fleet, as lettering and numerals were brought up to date. On the bus side, standardisation began on locally-built Daimlers with preselective gearboxes and, for many years, AEC engines. Mr Fearnley retired in 1962, and shortly afterwards the undertaking switched to rear-engined buses. The first batch comprised Leyland Atlanteans, which caused a furore in the city; subsequent double-deckers were all Daimler Fleetlines. Over 100 front-engined Daimlers, representing around a third of the fleet, still survived when Coventry Corporation Transport was absorbed into the West Midlands PTE on 1 April 1974, upon local government reorganisation. No doubt the accountants could draw some economy from this action but, from a transportation logic, it was a pointless move towards remoter control because the 'Meriden Gap' green belt has kept Coventry separate from the rest of the conurbation.

World War 2 brought disaster to Coventry and its transport department in November 1940, when the city was devastated by enemy bombers, rendering the tramway system unworkable and damaging many buses. Birmingham was actually bombed more than any other provincial city, but the raid on smaller Coventry was particularly notable for its concentration — indeed the word 'Coventrated', to describe massive devastation by bombing, was

Right: In 1957/8 three 1948/9 S8 buses received S15 front ends, complete with power doors and cab access via the saloon, bringing them right up to date. The tired brown upholstery was replaced by red, the completed package evidently being considered good enough for the long X96 service. No 3241 (JHA 841) passes through Dudley *en route* to Northampton. The bus ran until 1966, but latterly on less glamorous work. *Peter Yeomans*

coined during the war. Midland Red suffered little damage because, rather surprisingly, it did not have a garage in the city. Nevertheless, the company's crews and vehicles, already burdened by the need to move people in and out of the city each day on war production work, found demand massively increased by those bombed out of their homes or anxious to sleep somewhere perceived as safer.

After Coventry, the X96 moved on towards Rugby, taking around three quarters of an hour to reach the town famous for the 'modifications' to the rules of football introduced by one of its youths in 1823. It had a Midland Red garage so clearly adorned with the company's name that it could not be missed by users of the main-line railway station across the road.

The final leg to Northampton took a further hour. Northampton Corporation Transport's fleet was just under a hundred strong. The earlier choice of Thornycroft, Guy and then Crossley vehicles was, in time (following a trial vehicle in 1936), completely overtaken by a fine fleet of Daimlers. The 1939 batch had Roe bodies, and this combination became standard from 1949 until the last CVG6 models in 1968.

The Midland Red timetable showed connections at Northampton to Bedford and on to Cambridge, these being services of Eastern National until transferred in a rationalisation exercise to United Counties in 1952. United Counties was the principal company operator in Northampton and had its Head Office in the town. Being a Tilling and then a British Transport Commission company, United Counties was required to buy Eastern Coach Works-bodied Bristols and, by 1959, the entire fleet consisted of this combination. As such, the fleet held negligible interest for me, I suspect because I considered the principle of compulsory 'choice' disagreeable, as if Bristol could not compete with manufacturers like Leyland, which had supplied some of the BTC companies before nationalisation. Worse still, they were painted in Tilling green, a shade I never liked and an early example of corporate livery, although I can happily run my eye over Bristol/ ECW vehicles in Tilling red, Midland General blue or Scottish Bus Group liveries. All this was very unfair on United Counties, where the wide range of Bristol vehicles was much more varied than the Daimler/Roe standardisation of Northampton Corporation.

I mentioned in the Introduction that Banbury was not easy to reach by bus from Birmingham, and the X96 came in handy as a partial means of getting there. Service 511 linked Rugby with Banbury on Thursdays but at difficult times. More promisingly, service 509 linked Coventry with Banbury once a day on Thursdays and Fridays, and no fewer than four times on Saturdays — Banbury market days

were Thursday and Saturday. Even Northampton was linked by Midland Red to Banbury because the 512 linked the two twice on Wednesdays, thrice on Saturdays and once on Sunday evenings.

Having finally reached Banbury, the really adventurous could wander as far as Buckingham, linked to Banbury by a group of obscure routes, basically on Tuesdays and Saturdays. I now fear somebody will write to the publisher, pointing out that its idiot writer should have used route so-and-so linking Birmingham, Coventry, Leamington Spa and Banbury to Buckingham every 10 minutes. At both Banbury and Buckingham one could encounter the AECs of City of Oxford. These were beautifully painted and maintained, but the 1960s saw the company beset by loss of staff to car plants, just like Midland Red, and the sudden decline was just as tragic.

On our first visit to Banbury, we had difficulty locating the garage but, despite the twists and turns of our route in the drenching rain, we were followed everywhere by a brass band. Feeling persecuted, we were relieved to find the garage and not be pursued right into it, as stealth is a major part of any schoolboy's armoury. Try convincing the depot engineer that it's safe to let you wander about spotting the allocation while a brass band, apparently on close escort duty, plays the 'Radetzky March' at your elbow. Childhood horrors can stay with you a long time, and it was some years before I could comfortably go near a brass band again . . .

Above: A total of 219 S14s sounds like a big fleet of standard vehicles. However, the class contained many buses with experimental fittings, including 4313 with roll-over ventilators at Banbury in June 1970. S14 production was spread between 1955 and 1959, and withdrawal between 1967 and 1971. *Maurice Collignon*

Right: Coventry Corporation Manager Ronald Fearnley's apparent liking for AEC technology was frustrated when the AEC engine option was removed from the Daimler range, built in the city. The fact that the AEC Regent III, when fitted with the preselector gearbox, was probably the finest city bus of its time must have added to the frustration. AEC, however, had bought Maudslay, which had connections with the city. A one-off exercise was therefore for nine Regent IIIs to be assembled at Maudslay's Alcester works and badged as Maudslays; they entered service in January 1951 with Metro-Cammell bodies. No 125 is seen in Broadgate, 13 years later. *T. W. Moore*

Left: The same location, but in August 1973 the Gardner-engined Daimler is firmly in control. The CVG6 with Metro-Cammell Orion body was standard between 1955 and 1963 and, after a controversial order for Leyland Atlanteans, Daimler Fleetlines then ruled the roost. Bodywork on the Fleetlines was more varied, but East Lancs, including a few built by its subsidiary Neepsend, won most orders, as seen here. CVG6 298 and Fleetline 18 head the line in the latest livery, which had recently replaced the very attractive but more complex arrangement of the same colours carried by CVG6 318 behind. At the rear is one of the 41-58 batch of Fleetlines in the first livery for rear-engined vehicles, which employed the more conservative shades worn by Maudslay 125. *Malcolm Keeley*

Left: Low winter sun late in the day highlights passengers aboard 1952 BMMO S13 3905 at Pool Meadow, Coventry, preparing to travel to Rugby via Dunchurch in March 1966. It was late in the day for the S13 too, as most were withdrawn that year. The S13 was the first class of dual-purpose (bus/coach) vehicles, hence the black roof. The body on this one was built by Brush.
Malcolm Keeley collection

Right: Not all wartime Guys had austerity bodywork of dubious quality. Coventry Corporation 305 was a 1943 Guy Arab I with a steel-framed body begun by Metro-Cammell for Manchester Corporation, but set aside for war work until passing to its partner Weymann for finishing. It is pictured in Siskin Drive in 1959 on one of Coventry's many works services. *T. W. Moore*

Below left: SON 2197 (EHA 765) of 1938 stands outside Rugby's well-advertised garage. None of this batch of 50 buses was included in the extensive body-renovation programme of the early postwar period, suggesting that their English Electric bodies were not too bad; they lasted until 1952-6. Double-deckers could not run from this garage until March 1967, when its rebuilding was completed. *The Omnibus Society*

Below right: Coventry received around 100 austerity buses following the 1940 devastation and the loss of its tramway network. Numerically the last was 386, a Duple-bodied Daimler CWA6 actually delivered in peacetime, in 1946. It was extensively rebuilt by Bond in 1953, and is seen here, well laden on a morning works service, at Pool Meadow in 1958. Midland Red buses crowd the background. *T. W. Moore*

Left: Roe-bodied Daimlers leave Northampton Corporation's St James' garage in June 1959. No 194 (DNH 194) is a 1953 CVG6, while 106 (VV 8202) is a 1939 COG5. *T. W. Moore*

Below left: It is still surprising that Midland Red's territory was so vast that it encountered Red Rover of Aylesbury's buses at Buckingham. Red Rover was fond of the London Transport RT class, but No 8 (FXT 206) was of particular interest as one of the few 'prewar' RTs to run for another operator. Midland Red S15 4612 of Banbury garage occupies the background in this March 1958 scene. *Roy Marshall*

Below right: Plymouth Corporation bought six Crossley DD42/5 models in 1948, complete with Crossley 53-seat lowbridge bodies. Being non-standard, they were sold in 1958, and four found their way into the fleet of Wesley, Stoke Goldington. Three came via other operators, but Wesley's 24 (DJY 963) came direct from the dealer and was fitted with platform doors by its new operator; it ran until 1964. A BMMO S14 lurks behind the Crossley at Northampton in April 1959. *Richard Butler*

Left: United Counties' standardisation on Bristol/ECW vehicles was spoiled by the takeovers of Birch Bros' stage services in 1969 and Luton Corporation in 1970, and the situation was never retrieved. Ex-Birch 1962 Leyland Leopard/Willowbrook 235 (82 CYV), looking very similar to a Midland Red LS18, stands in Northampton bus station in July 1974. *Malcolm Keeley*

Above: Midland Red D7 4086, looking a little jaded, prepares for a journey from Banbury on service 490 to Adderbury West, while a City of Oxford AEC Reliance occupies the background. *Chris Aston*

Lasses and Leylands to Leamington

One of my ways of occupying myself for an afternoon in school holidays was to go LD8 riding. These 100 Leyland Titan PD2s made a quite different sound from virtually anybody else's Leylands, and their standard Leyland bodies were disguised — but arguably not improved — by BMMO-style fronts. Conductors were not keen on them because of their low seat-backs, but drivers loved the part-synchromesh gearboxes and big engines that made them fly. My local Birmingham garage, Digbeth, had 35 of these beasts, so there was always a good chance one would turn up, and it was a sad day when the last one at Digbeth was retired in May 1967. Another garage well-endowed with LD8s was Leamington, Myton Road, and very well maintained they were too. My trip was therefore usually around the triangle created by Birmingham, Stratford-upon-Avon and Coventry.

To be precise the jaunt would begin in Shirley, on the boundary with Birmingham's Hall Green. The company contemplated a garage at Shirley in the heady days after World War 2, which would have suited me mightily, but it never came to pass. Service 150 to Stratford was very popular on Sundays and Bank Holidays if I chose to travel on those days, but Midland Red never let me down; there was always

a duplicate if required. There was a minor gnashing of teeth, however, if a BMMO D7 came along — these lightweights were not popular among my circle of friends, being described perceptively as 'pop rivets and hardboard' by one. In earlier years the company would happily send out three double-deckers non-stop from Birmingham Bull Ring to Stratford with only one conductor, even if the buses were open-platform. Double-deck PMT buses on its X1 service had a break several hours long at Digbeth, and they would also be pressed into use, sometimes without asking the owners first!

Encounters with Leylands increased at Stratford, because this was the home of Stratford Blue. I was astonished to learn this little company had been a wholly-owned subsidiary of Midland Red since 1935 — there was absolutely no evidence of it in the look of the fleet. Secondhand Tilling-Stevens buses had been swept away after World War 2 by a new fleet of Leylands, beautifully kept in subtle shades of blue and cream, the double-deckers being set off by a silver roof. I would have more readily accepted Stratford Blue as a subsidiary of, say, Yorkshire Traction, on account of its vehicle policy.

Stratford Blue seemed to have a vast territory for a small fleet of around 40 buses and, indeed, should one have wanted to extend one's use of a 'Day Anywhere' ticket southwesterly to the next Midland Red town of note, Evesham, then one would have had difficulty. Astonishingly, one was not allowed to use 'Day Anywhere' tickets on the BMMO subsidiary, including its workings on service 150, until the end of 1963, when the price increased from 10s (50p) to 12s 6d (62.5p), and one could then use them on Stratford Blue services, except between Long Compton and Oxford on the joint service 44 with City of Oxford.

Stratford Blue largely had Stratford to Evesham sewn up with its generally hourly 5/5A. Midland Red linked the two twice a day with the marathon X91 Leicester–Hereford service. Another, very attractive possibility was service 524 via Mickleton, Chipping Campden and Broadway. It took 82-85 minutes but followed a splendid route through the best of the Cotswolds. Your writer has a soft spot for Chipping Campden, which is where my branch of the Keeleys came from. I grew up to believe all countryside looked like the Cotswolds, and it still sets the standard in my mind. A shop in Chipping Campden actually bears the Keeley name, and a look at the war memorial in the church is a sobering reminder of why my family seemed short of relatives. It is today hard to believe the village was not built as part of a countryside theme park, but I remember it before 'gentrification' really took hold. Despite its obvious charms today, country life for most had been for centuries little more than grinding poverty and backbreaking labour. It remained sufficiently so at the

Below: Stratford Blue is associated prewar with secondhand Tilling-Stevens buses, replaced postwar by new Leylands. There were other makes, however. Midland Red took over the Worcestershire fleet of P. Owen & Sons, Abberley, in November 1938, and transferred to Stratford Blue two Maudslay ML3s with W. D. Smith 32-seat coach bodies. No 21 (WP 3425) dated from 1933 and is seen in Stratford's former bus station alongside the 'Red Lion' public house. The two Maudslays were retained until 1946. *R. T. Wilson, courtesy BaMMOT*

Left: Amongst the many secondhand Tilling-Stevens B10A2 buses were 16 1930 ex-West Yorkshire examples with this style of bodywork built by Tilling, United or Roe, purchased in October 1938. Tilling-bodied No 5 (WX 2120) stands in the bus station, with the almost inevitable advertisement for the local brewery. This bus was to be the last of the 16 when withdrawn in February 1949. *R. T. Wilson, courtesy BaMMOT*

dawn of the 20th century to drive my grandfather to follow so many of his ancestors to one of the big cities, in his case Birmingham and employment with the Great Western Railway. In due course, my grandfather married and was able to afford a house in Birmingham, where he created a beautiful garden so full of Cotswold stone that it looked like an outstation of Hidcote Manor. Too late now to ask Grandad whether he would have liked to have returned home to Campden, but I suspect cherishing that garden was too much to give up. Even at the age of 90, he delighted in showing off his garden, especially to 'young' ladies, the adjective being applied to any girl under the age of 80. The old boy effortlessly charmed ladies of any age, including my wife, with his twinkling eyes and Cotswold accent — an enviable performance.

My afternoon jaunts mostly pre-dated the inclusion of Stratford Blue in the 'Day Anywhere' ticket, so instead I would go north towards Coventry on a network of routes via Warwick and/or Leamington Spa. These routes were firmly in the grip of Midland Red's two Leamington garages, and I would not have to wait long for an LD8, preferably on the X90, which was the direct route to Coventry. Heavy traffic was always present at weekends in the area, and the LD8s were well equipped to make up lost time. The company had a perennial problem with driver shortages at Leamington; hired buses and drivers of private operators with Midland Red conductors were a familiar sight on these routes. One of my journeys had a Leyland PD2 of a very different mechanical specification, being an ex-London Transport RTL with preselector gearbox hired from G&G — a type which very briefly entered the Midland Red fleet after the 1974 takeover of Harper of Heath Hayes.

Like, I guess, most youths, I would relax on my bed, gazing at the ceiling and, as the teenage years clicked in, spending less time creating my perfect bus fleet and more on creating my own dream girl out of actresses I had seen on screen. My heroines were mostly brunettes with slightly more eye make-up than good taste permitted although, I have to say, there were fairer-haired exceptions. On one of my rainy day rides between Stratford and Coventry, the nearest creature to my dream girl sat down next to me — tight black raincoat,

Right: Classic Stratford Blue as Willowbrook-bodied Leyland PD3A/1 6 (673 HNX) stands in the garage yard at Stratford in April 1965. This batch of six, delivered in the winter of 1963/4, introduced a more modern fleetname, but the traditional silver roof survived until the next delivery. Stratford Blue built up a fleet of 15 PD3s, all 73-seaters, between 1960 and 1966, but Midland Red sold them all to Isle of Man Road Services in the early 1970s. *Malcolm Keeley*

Far right: Stratford Blue was absorbed into Midland Red on the first day of 1971. The four 1963 Leyland Titan PD3/4s with Northern Counties bodies were repainted red but did not receive any improvement to their destination displays. By the time this photograph was taken in August 1971, 536 EUE had become unmistakably Midland Red 2024 but, bearing in mind the number of services then using Birmingham's Bull Ring bus station, the destination without 150 service number is wonderfully vague. *Malcolm Keeley*

black hair and lovely blue eyes. I just had to engage her in conversation, because the entire path of my future surely hinged on it. Sophia Riggobrigida, shall we call her, was obviously older than me, and seemed to be returning from shopping — this was the time before the weekly sweep around the supermarket took away that almost daily practice. She was a young housewife, hopefully bored enough to want to brighten her day by seducing an off-duty schoolboy into adulthood. I needed a chat-up line — I needed at least 5% of Grandad's effortless charm. I decided a conversation on the relative merits of the D7 and LD8 would not do the trick. Instead I feigned absent-mindedness as to which of the many routes via Warwick and Leamington I was travelling on. Sophia turned to me with the sweetest and most genuine of smiles and told me which service I was enjoying, but the dancing look in her lovely eyes hinted that she realised I already knew the answer. My inexperience meant no hope of a follow-up and, not surprisingly, under-age seduction was not on her agenda that day. Shortly after, Sophia reached her stop and walked out of my life forever.

Service 159 would return me from Coventry to Birmingham. I aimed on weekdays for one particular evening-peak journey, which I knew was worked by Leamington garage (those Midland Red schedulers knew how to screw the last ounce of work out of vehicles and crews!), and thus had the best chance of an LD8. This coincided with factory finish time, and, without the aid of today's bypass, the bus would be seriously late by the time it reached the far end of

Allesley. The 159 was tightly timed, but the A45 had been rebuilt in the 1950s as a fast dual carriageway up to the Birmingham boundary. Even before the A45 reconstruction, however, it had to cope with a 58min journey time and only 2min layover to make up for lost time, go to the toilet or grab a cup of tea. Those LD8s would hammer along, only diverting from the modern dual carriageway to serve Meriden — a village used for manufacturer's photographs when the LD8s were new.

Meriden is the alleged geographical centre of England, which makes it the worst possible place to decide you want a stroll along the seashore. It stands at the foot of a steep hill, and one bus-driving friend, desperate for time, decided at the crest that it would be a good idea to knock his 159 out of gear to pick up a bit more speed. His bus was soon travelling alarmingly at the far side of 60mph, and re-engaging gear was out of the question. The brakes quickly faded as the bus rocked past the first two stops at the foot of the hill and finally rolled to a successful halt opposite the cyclists' memorial in the centre of the village. Digbeth drivers competed (obviously unofficially!) for the fastest time between Coventry and Birmingham. The idea was to leave Coventry as late as possible before the resident inspector went berserk and run early inside Birmingham where the Corporation picked up the local passengers. Another friend's fastest time was 35min with a D9 early one Sunday morning, an *average* speed of around 30mph. The 159, appropriately passing Birmingham airport, was definitely a route for flyers.

Right: Stratford-upon-Avon attracts big crowds on Bank Holidays, and in earlier times Midland Red ran substantial numbers of duplicates, which were parked up at Stratford until people started to return home. This 1960 line-up shows D7 4541 and AD2 3121 from the Leicester end of the X91, and then a number of Digbeth vehicles duplicating service 150, with D7 4442 and LD8 4011 nearest.
T. W. Moore

Left: Underfloor-engined BMMO D10 4943 was delivered to Digbeth on 10 January 1961 and placed in service that evening on the 159. It is seen here loading at Pool Meadow, Coventry, soon afterwards.
T. W. Moore Collection

Far left: The good old days? The petrol engine of 1932 REDD/Eastern Counties HA 8018 is started by muscle power on the handle at Pool Meadow, Coventry, before making the dash to Birmingham on service 159.
R. T. Wilson, courtesy BaMMOT

Left: The golden period for country living may have been the decades following World War 2. Poverty declined and today's curses of rising property prices, village facilities closing and the whole raft of farming economic ills had not begun. The icing on the cake would have been a silky ride home from shopping in Leamington Spa on a 1950 AD2-class AEC Regent II/Metro-Cammell like 3162 (JHA 63).
John Fozard

Midland Red S12 3751 works a local service through the Georgian centre of Leamington Spa in April 1965.
Martin Llewellyn

Lasses for this Leyland to Leamington. Willowbrook-bodied Leopard PSU3/4 5231 picks up passengers at Pool Meadow, Coventry, in June 1973; the poppy-red Leopard to the left reveals we are now entering the era of the NBC corporate livery. *T. W. Moore*

Right: Hutfield of Warwick supplied EUF 192, an ex-Southdown 1938 Leyland Titan TD5 with Beadle bodywork, seen ahead of a more typical LD8 Leyland on Midland Red's services out of Pool Meadow, Coventry. *T. W. Moore Collection*

Far right: An atmospheric picture showing three LD8s making their way south out of Coventry early one morning in November 1966. The first two are 4070 and 4059, but, most interesting, following is one of 4048 and 4055, the two LD8s sold to G&G, Leamington, for use on Midland Red services. *T. W. Moore*

Right: An early postwar view of Warwick Market Place, when the sun always shone and vehicles like relegated coach 1499 (HA 9051) ran Leamington and Warwick locals. This was the prototype LRR, built in 1933, relegated to a bus in 1941 and retired in 1950. *BaMMOT Collection*

Left: Evesham's spacious, tree-lined High Street was terminus to many Midland Red services serving the fertile Vale bearing the market town's name. S6 3090 of 1947 is seen early in life, before the balance of the design was improved by lengthening behind the rear axle. It was destined to be the first S6 to be withdrawn, at the end of 1960; the last, 3023, ran until 1965. Weston Subedge was a classic Grandad destination — is that his 1938 Ford Eight? *The Omnibus Society*

Far left: Anxiety attack. The driver of 1943 (CHA 2) looks down the bus with concern as it struggles to clear the queue at Warwick Market Place on the infrequent Birmingham service in July 1950. This was one of four rear-engined prototypes built in 1935-7 and extensively rebuilt during the war to underfloor-engine layout as prototypes for the postwar fleet, being reclassified S1 to S4. A further, all-new prototype followed — a chassisless bus designated S5; chassisless construction would become standard for BMMO products from the S14. The five prototypes were withdrawn between 1956 and 1958. No 1943 was the S3 and displays much of the styling employed from the S6 onwards, but the proportions had yet to be perfected. It was unique amongst BMMO-manufactured vehicles in having a preselective gearbox, like Daimlers, which is probably why it spent much of its underfloor-engined career working out of Birmingham's Digbeth garage.
T. W. Moore collection

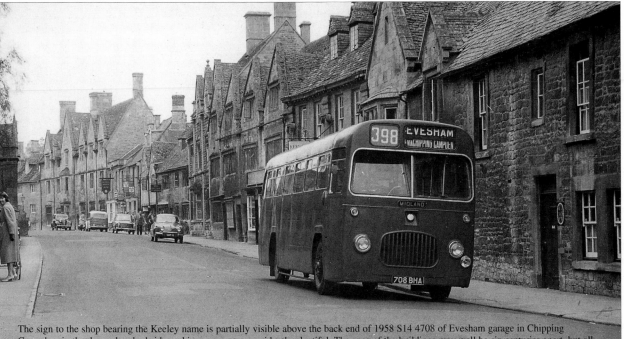

The sign to the shop bearing the Keeley name is partially visible above the back end of 1958 S14 4708 of Evesham garage in Chipping Campden, in the days when kerbside parking spaces were evidently plentiful. The ages of the buildings may well be six centuries apart, but all sit together cohesively. *Robert F. Mack*

Far left: Midland Red's later Alexander-bodied Daimler Fleetlines had separate centre exits which were rarely used in practice. No 6182, one of 70 new in 1969, works through the centre of Kenilworth in April 1971, pursued by an E-type Jaguar. The final batch of 33, built in 1970/1 with J-suffix registrations, all seemed to include a severed rivet-head trapped inside the overhead grabrail, which ran the length of the lower saloon. Every time the bus braked or accelerated, the rivet-head would go rinky-dink-a-dink from one end of the bus to the other — massively irritating on any long journey of, say, over 200 yards. *Martin Llewellyn*

Left: Give my regards to Broadway. BMMO S17 5615, two months old but still looking very new in April 1965, passes through the lovely Cotswold village of that name rather than its marginally better-known but heavily urbanised New York namesake. The village is aptly named, with its wide, mile-long main street of mellow honey-coloured stone buildings and walls. *Chris Aston*

91

Worcester: Source of Interest

Above: The 143 ran from Birmingham to Bromsgrove via Rednal and the Lickeys, where this picture was taken, almost certainly in 1950. Adequate supplies of fresh air into the upper saloons of the early postwar double-deckers evidently soon caused concern, and 1949 BMMO D5 3478 has experimental ventilators in the front windows. This was not the favoured solution — the D1 prototype, AD2s and D5s, always slightly worried in appearance, soon received ventilators above the front windows which made them look positively anxious. Hopper ventilators became standard on the D7s onwards, funnelling flies into the upper saloon on warm days until mesh was fitted to sieve all but the smallest! No 3478 was withdrawn in 1963, a bad year for this first batch of D5s, although a few hung on until 1966. *Michael Rooum*

Birmingham is right in the middle of the country, and whether all Birmingham preferred to look southwest for its pleasures in the days before overseas travel is arguable, but south-side Brummies certainly did. Residents on the north side of the city showed an apparent reluctance to cross 'town', which meant the attractions of resorts like those in North Wales were stiff competition for those beyond Bristol. Midland Red's immaculate red and black coaches were to be found busily meeting any of these demands, as well as providing up-market tours throughout the British Isles. In the earlier half of the 20th century, however, many could not afford to travel any further southwest than the Corporation tram ride to Rednal to enjoy a day in the Lickey Hills, just across the boundary. The Rednal tram route did incredible business, but, travelling further in the same direction, so did Midland Red's service 144 to Worcester and the Malverns, patronised by those with just a little more money in their pockets and, perhaps, a 'Day Anywhere' ticket.

The 144, terminating at Malvern Wells, took around 2hr 20min to complete the journey. It ran every 20min, including Sundays, increased to every 15min on Saturdays, and double-deckers were standard. In addition, holiday periods would see considerable duplication. Just as Midland Red was ready on the first day of the M1 with new motorway coaches to London, the first day of the M5 on 20 July 1962 saw motorway express services introduced between Birmingham and Worcester. This reduced the journey time between the two cities from 93min to 50min, faster than the then rail services. Midland Red took further advantage of the M5 in November 1965, when a new link road at Quinton permitted half the Worcester expresses to be diverted via Bearwood as service X43. Since then the railways have got their act together and the motorway service has ceased, but happily the 144 lives on, although today it ventures beyond Worcester to the Malverns only on Sundays.

Worcester was an important centre for the company. It obtained a ready-made network in Worcester (and Kidderminster) when fellow BET company Worcestershire Motor Transport had many of its buses commandeered by the Government for troop transport during World War 1, and Midland Red had to step in. It was also the starting-place for Midland Red's letter-prefixed local services when the company's buses replaced the city's tramcars on 1 June 1928. The successful agreement between the company and the Corporation was used in many other places, well beyond Midland Red territory — 'Worcester Agreement' terms became a useful shorthand description in the industry. A large fleet of single-deckers maintained the local services until 1986, when deregulation ushered in the era of the minibus. In addition, a wide selection of Midland Red country services

connected the county town with outlying villages and adjacent towns, working out of the former Newport Street bus station alongside the River Severn, the buses occasionally being displaced by flooding.

While the 144 to the Malverns was one option, other Birmingham–Worcester services continued well into the territories of the nationalised Bristol Tramways and its subsidiaries. These were the X72, which continued to Gloucester, and the X73/74 to Cheltenham. Bristol's Bristols had the same problem for me as United Counties': they were clad in Tilling green. The buses operating Gloucester's city services were separate from the main country fleet and were marked as such. The Cheltenham District subsidiary, however, retained a delightful non-Tilling livery of dark red and cream, and, despite its relatively small size, the fleet was a splendid example of the effects of ownership on vehicle-buying policy. It had passed through Balfour Beatty and Red & White ownership before nationalisation had seen it placed under Bristol Tramways management. In my Midland Red 'Day Anywhere' days, Cheltenham District could still boast Albion and Guy vehicles dating from its Red & White era, but the prewar AECs of its Balfour Beatty period had long gone.

Left: One of the last repaints with traditional transfers was D7 4538 of Worcester garage, seen at Malvern Wells terminus on 13 June 1970. The cautionary washing advice notice applied to repaints remains on the cab door. The traditional 'MIDLAND' illuminated sign below the front upper-deck windows has been painted over to prevent any possible confusion with 'pay as you enter' illuminated signs then being fitted to one-man-operated vehicles. Passengers endeavouring to pay D7 drivers would have been an interesting sight. On Bank Holidays in earlier times the path stretching up behind 4538 would have been crammed with people queuing to return to Birmingham. *Malcolm Keeley*

Above: 5557 was an interesting S17 because, following fire damage, it was rebuilt with S23 body parts, most noticeably the peaked roof. It is seen here in Edgbaston Street, Birmingham, having turned right out of the Bull Ring bus station in June 1973, *en route* to Redditch on service 142 via Rednal and Barnt Green. By this date it has the grey wheels required by National Bus Company corporate-livery edict, but the remainder of the bus awaits a visit to Central Works to receive NBC poppy red. *Malcolm Keeley*

Right: The Birmingham–Selly Oak–Worcester X44 motorway service via the new M5 opened for business on 20 July 1962. The scene is Dudley Street, Birmingham, with the new Bull Ring centre well underway behind. CM5 4834 is very close to the entrance of the new Midland Red bus station, eventually opened on 1 November 1963. The CM5 driver has a coachman's white coat; another driver in standard summerweight jacket passes comment through the open window. No 4834 was built in 1961 as an ordinary C5 coach, the 8-litre engine being modified to CM5 turbocharged form for this service. Like most of the C5 family, 4834 was withdrawn in 1971, but the class lives on as a Corgi model. *Malcolm Keeley collection*

Below left: The massive Austin motor works at Longbridge was a busy place at shift-change times. No 2148 (EHA 280) works service 332 to Bromsgrove; only the lower deck has required rebuilding on this 1938 Brush-bodied FEDD. A BMMO S9 waits behind while a Birmingham City Transport 1951 Daimler CVD6 (one of Yardley Wood's allocation, 2071-2100) lurks to work a journey over service 18A. One of Austin's own lorries passes by. *Michael Rooum*

Left: The C5 family was soon rendered obsolete by revised dimensions allowing 36ft length and greater capacity. The company built one more generation of purpose-built motorway coaches, the 30-strong CM6 class; the 1963 prototype was followed by the production vehicles in 1965/6. Five, 5667-71, were built without toilets for the Birmingham–Worcester services. While many C5 coaches were relegated to bus work, only 5654 of the CM6s was refitted as such, in 1971. It is seen here at Worcester's Newport Street bus station in July of that year. These vehicles quickly accrued high mileages, and were withdrawn between 1972 and 1974. *Malcolm Keeley*

Above: A wonderfully animated scene at Worcester's Newport Street bus station on a very busy day in 1946. Midland Red crews discuss the next activities of OLR coach-to-bus conversion 1691 (AHA 636), intended for service W29 to Hallow, and SON 1892 (CHA 516), working the 308 to Stockton-on-Teme, but a substantial number of passengers on the right remains to be moved. *Ian Allan Library*

97

Far left: Midland Red 4255 has had a charmed life. It was the second production S14 and entered service at Worcester in April 1955. It moved to Leamington in 1963, and again to Malvern in 1967, by which time it was becoming a candidate for retirement. Instead, in 1968, it was overhauled again, despite being one of the few S14s not converted for one-person operation. It became a 'float' vehicle, moving from garage to garage as required, before finally returning to Worcester, where it was withdrawn in November 1970. It is seen here in Worcester's Newport Street bus station in June of that year and has obviously suffered from boiling up. It covered over half a million miles during its service life, and fortunately passed into preservation. It is now part of the BaMMOT collection at Wythall. *Malcolm Keeley*

Left: The creeping 'Bristolisation' of Cheltenham District is reflected by Bristol KSW PHW 991. New in 1953 as No 87 in the Cheltenham fleet, it became 8558 when the subsidiary's buses were renumbered into the main Bristol series in 1966. The service to Benhall was previously numbered 4, but had become 592 by the time of this June 1969 view of a deserted town centre, many years before Sunday trading became legal. The traditional Cheltenham District livery would survive for a little longer. *Malcolm Keeley*

Go West, Young Man

On the western flank of Midland Red's territory was another fine ride through two of England's least spoilt counties, Herefordshire and Shropshire. This was the X34 or X35 between Hereford, Leominster, Ludlow and Shrewsbury, the two service numbers representing variations in villages served *en route*. In Herefordshire the buses worked through genial countryside permitting the production of hops and cider, and heather- and gorse-clad hills at the northern end. Today the timbered dwellings dating back to the 15th and 16th centuries and spectacular castles can still be enjoyed, but not from a Midland Red double-decker.

The postwar travel boom generated sufficient trade on this pair of services to warrant double-deckers, which operated hourly (having been reduced to approximately three-hourly with saloons during the war), with an end-to-end time of 2hr 50min. Hereford and Shrewsbury are both substantial towns affording bus garages with, in those days, unchallenging local services that could provide a haven for less nimble buses such as the AD2 class. Attractive Ludlow used to have its own little garage and offered cause for a break almost exactly halfway along the journey. Far from enjoying a relaxed existence, Ludlow's vehicles for many years actually covered a greater daily mileage than any others in the fleet, no doubt due to its country routes with faster timings and high off-peak vehicle utilisation. It was perhaps an unexpected outpost of the LD8 class, and these took their place alongside BMMO types on the X34/35.

The X34/35 would promise a fast run, apart from the odd village diversion, bowling along the A49 amidst the Leyland Octopus, AEC Mammoth, Scammell and other heavy lorries trunking between the North West and South Wales or the West Country. The motorway network has relieved the A49, but the principal towns are still beset by the continual growth in car demand. The early postwar years saw the introduction of flat-rate road tax instead of tax based on horsepower, which had led to many underpowered cars on the road. These slow-revving designs were around for many years afterwards, however, and the typical BMMO or LD8 was more than a match for them. Many a Standard or Morris Eight owner out on the open road such as the A49 must have looked in the rear mirror and seen nothing but the grin of a BMMO grille filling the view. Not that the buses of the time had themselves progressed fully along the evolutionary chain, and the LD8 combined a powerful engine with primitive braking and a high centre of gravity, compared to buses of today. A friend with considerable bus-driving experience recalls, with the amused stiff-upper-lip gravity shown by survivors of terrifying ordeals, his white-knuckle LD8 ride on the X35. His smile competes with the astonishment still in his eyes after all these years as he describes how the driver hurled his steed around the narrow streets and corners of the towns and villages *en route*, not least the steep gradients through Ludlow. The ride terminated with the driver, as a final gesture of contempt for his employers, silencing the engine at Hereford by stalling the bus on the clutch rather than using the approved method.

Many small independents disappeared over the years, but generally they survived best in the areas between the big operators, and this is very true of the Welsh borders. Midland Red crews could exchange news with Red & White colleagues at Hereford, but barely encountered those of Crosville, the next major operator to the north on the Welsh side. Herefordshire and Shropshire thus had a strong presence of independents, and, whilst the typical elderly Bedford was

ever present, there were also strands of highly independent thought in vehicle purchasing. Red & White also had distinctive views, and, even when the Albions, Guys and Leylands were swept aside by post-nationalisation Bristols, the company managed to maintain some mystique. It also helped, in my case, that they were painted red, not green!

Access to the X34/35 corridor from Birmingham could be gained from two directions, via the X96 to Shrewsbury or the 192 to Ludlow. There was also the more obscure and circuitous 190 to Ludlow, referred to earlier in this book. Hereford was a problem, as no suitable link existed; there was a 409 service which ran early on a Sunday, taking until lunchtime to reach Hereford and then returning in the evening, but that did not provide a productive day for us. Today, I am pleased to see the 192 still runs between Birmingham and Ludlow but additionally now covers the southern end of the long-deceased X34/35 to Hereford.

Reference to the exceptionally long X96, operated every four hours, has already been made in the Northampton chapter. The normal story, after my time, is one of frequency decline on many routes, but the X96 was joined in September 1967 by additional variants X93/94/95 between Coventry and Shrewsbury, no doubt influenced by the development of Telford. Riding the X96 felt a bit special, its sheer distance, low frequency and long sections of country running giving it a pioneering Wells Fargo air — an unfair description, because it enjoyed the best dual-purpose-seated vehicles.

An interesting arrangement of independent bus operators, the Shropshire Omnibus Association, existed around Wellington, running a network of services as a co-operative venture, and gave additional reason to pause there. The development of Telford should

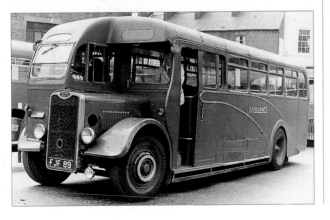

have boosted their fortunes but, rather surprisingly, the Association sold its bus services in 1978 to Midland Red.

The 192 Birmingham–Ludlow service runs via Kidderminster and Bewdley. Midland Red ran a very good frequency (15 or 20min, depending on period) between Birmingham and Kidderminster, with half the buses continuing on to Bewdley as service 132, the remainder continuing to Stourport as service 133. As usual, Midland Red timetable-planners had a good grip on demand and resources because, on weekdays, the 192 would be low-frequency with, typically, four journeys each way on what would normally be service 132 timings extended to and from Ludlow. The 192 primarily appealed to the leisure market, so the weekend timetable was quite different, with the 192 operating mostly hourly as a separate service and trailing a 132, which cleared the shorter-distance demand out of Birmingham. Ludlow was not necessarily the end of the line, however, because for many years there was a summer-only X92 service continuing to Llandrindod Wells.

Double-deckers were introduced to the 192 in May 1950, no doubt after frenzied activity by a tree-cutting vehicle, and for some years LD8s migrated from Bearwood to Ludlow to boost the summer double-deck allocation there. Passengers were able to see over the hedgerows, enjoying splendid countryside, and the delights of towns and villages en route, such as Bewdley, Cleobury Mortimer and Ludlow itself. The top of Clee Hill, over 1,250ft above sea level, was arguably the best view from any Midland Red bus route. There were

Left: The two 1949 Barnard-bodied Guy Arab IIIs taken over from Kemp & Shaw in 1959 drifted away to Shropshire (one at Shrewsbury and one at Ludlow), where they caused havoc with their non-standard destination displays — boards had probably disappeared with the prewar vehicles. How archaic they looked amongst a single-decker fleet that had been entirely underfloor-engined since the withdrawal of the last SON in 1958. No 4842 (FJF 89) manœuvres at Shrewsbury in 1961; the two were withdrawn the following year. Note the use of a smaller fleetname, necessitated by the trim.
Malcolm Keeley collection

Above: Hereford bus station in 1967, and smart 1961 C5 coach 4821 stands alongside Ludlow garage's new S21 5857, the latter's semi-coach status still permitting it a black roof. Nos 5860 onwards would wear a short-lived maroon in *lieu* of black, but all-over red would not be long behind. No 5857 is bound for Shrewsbury, but the distinguished X35 status has been replaced by 435. Limited-stop services were then being introduced around the system using the 'X' prefix, and several existing 'X' services, lengthy but not limited-stop, were renumbered into the main series. *Tennent's Trains, Halesowen*

Right: D7s continued to receive the splendid old-style gold transfers until June 1970, and few were repainted after then. No 4503, outside St Peter's Church, Hereford, on 13 June 1970, was thus a rare recipient of this style of lettering and rarer still in this dull gold, as a bolder style with yellow edged in black and repositioned fleetnumbers was thankfully introduced in October of that year. No 4503, first licensed on 1 July 1956, was the first D7 to be allocated from new to Hereford and remained there all its life, giving it a fairly relaxed existence. The only other D7 allocated from new to Hereford was 4750, still working from Hereford that June day in 1970 and looking in just as good order as 4503. Despite the repaint, 4503 was withdrawn in November 1970. *Malcolm Keeley*

spectacular first-gear climbs at the Ludlow end of the route; the BMMO crash gearbox was a relatively quiet affair, but one certainly recognised the first ratio, with its pronounced whine. The hills meant it was a route that a driver needed to treat with the greatest respect, not least the dip at Hopton Wafers where the double bend at the foot of significant gradients, and probably a waiting passenger, meant no chance of taking a run at the uphill sections on either side. Another friend, driving a Leyland Leopard coach for a private operator on an excursion to Ludlow, had brake failure on the bends at Hopton Wafers. Ashen-faced, and perhaps unwisely, he crept on down to Ludlow using the handbrake and engine as a brake, and phoned home base for a change vehicle. His normally polite demeanour disappeared when he was asked if he could nurse the coach and passengers back home!

Right: 'Day Anywhere' rides were a pleasant way to spend a summer day, but Midland Red buses were hard at work through all the seasons. The windows are steamed up and the crew is probably perishing in the cold as S10 3604 provides part of the frequent service between Birmingham and Kidderminster, and beyond, one snowy day *circa* 1954. Behind is a rare Austin A70 with pick-up bodywork by Jensen. These early postwar S-types gave around 15 years of service, but 3604 was unfortunate, being destroyed by fire in 1956 and having by far the shortest life of them all. *Ian Allan Library*

Left: Yeoman's Motors of Canon Pyon was another business developed in the 1920s. It expanded considerably during World War 2 due to airfield construction. Double-deckers were introduced in 1940, employing initially ex-Glasgow Leyland Titan TD1s and a rare AEC Q, ex-Birmingham. Yeoman's evidently became fond of the side-engined AEC Q, HF 9401 being one of two 1934 examples with Roe 56-seat bodies purchased from Wallasey in 1946. Alongside at Hereford bus station is DCJ 300, a Daimler CWA6 with Duple 53-seat lowbridge bodywork, delivered new to Yeomans in 1945. From the late 1950s Yeoman's would obtain registration numbers ending in 00 for all vehicles purchased new, but the CWA6 was long gone by then. *R. A. Mills*

Above left: A Midland Red single-decker is glimpsed through the shelters under construction behind Red & White 1935 Albion Valiant/ Northern Counties 256 at Hereford bus station around 1950. The Albion was sold in 1952. *S. E. Letts*

Left: The interesting fleet of Bengry of Leominster traded as Primrose Motor Services. GVJ 880 was a 1950 Foden PVSC6 which ran for Bengry for 10 years before sale to a contractor. The smart Foden front end was sadly often bodied by ill-proportioned products of small coachbuilders, but here the job was entrusted to Burlingham, which did its usual handsome work. Jammed half-drop windows are a sign that, in this case, the body is getting tired. The Foden waits in Leominster bus station, ready for a run to Kington. *Alan D. Broughall*

Right: Three S9s, 3372/4/85, were converted to attractive tree-cutting vehicles in 1963. No 3385 was allocated to Hereford garage and is seen in 1967.
Tennent's Trains, Halesowen

Far right: BMMO S22 5906 begins its long journey on service X94 to Wellington in August 1973. Coventry Daimler CVG6 292 follows it out of that city's Pool Meadow bus station.
Malcolm Keeley

Right: Never mind the quality, feel the width. Brand-new S8/Metro-Cammell 3234 (JHA 834) loads at Shrewsbury on 18 July 1948 for Northampton. Later models would have dual-purpose bus/coach seating for such a long run, but the passengers were nevertheless enjoying one of the company's first eight-footers; until 1950, operators had to seek permission from relevant authorities to run 8ft-wide buses on specified routes. Alongside is one of the last batch of SONs, built in 1940 with more rounded bodywork by Brush. Hopefully the crew of 2403 (GHA 322) will remember the destination board before moving off. *S. L. Smith*

Right: The buses of Mid-Wales Motorways of Newtown were familiar in Shrewsbury for many years and included double-deckers, but the fleet was legendary for its elderly Bedfords. This atmospheric view, taken in March 1959, shows 1937 WTB AAW 238, with Duple body rebuilt by the operator in 1950 when newly acquired from France of Llanymynech. *Richard Butler*

Left: You can't tell it's Butter. This petrol-engined Guy Vixen with Barnard 29-seat coachwork displaying rather faded ownership and registration details belonged to Butter of Childs Ercall. FAW 725 was seen in Shrewsbury in March 1959. *Richard Butler*

Far left: For many years H. Brown & Sons of Donnington Wood ran a fleet of rare Sentinels, but this Vulcan 6PF is even rarer. Vulcan, originally based in Southport, was purchased in 1937 by Maidstone-based Tilling-Stevens, which transferred van and lorry production to Maidstone. Manufacture of bus and coach chassis ceased until this design was introduced at the end of 1949, when this bus was new. Fitted with Perkins P6 4.73-litre diesel engines, a number were sold to small independents until production again ceased in 1951 following the Rootes Group's purchase of Vulcan and Tilling-Stevens the previous year. Obscure chassis attracted obscure bodies; FAW 967 at Oakengates received Dutfield coachwork, and had only a few more months to run in March 1959. *Richard Butler*

Below: Although Sentinel was not far behind BMMO in introducing underfloor-engined single-deckers, it did not manage to take advantage of its lead over the big manufacturers. This Salopia Sentinel was significant, being the first of the underfloor-engined breed. The arrangement of open front entrance with hinged door to the saloon in the front bulkhead was the same as that on the contemporary BMMO S6 model. Sentinel was based in Shrewsbury, where this picture of EUJ 792 was taken in March 1959, and Salopia in Whitchurch. The 40-seat body was by Beadle. *Richard Butler*

Right: Wellington-allocated BMMO S16 5125 works the Bridgnorth town service in May 1973. *Malcolm Keeley*

Far right: As our tour of Midland Red's territory draws to a close, we must acknowledge the company's fine coaches which could turn up anywhere. No 4209, one of a batch of 63 Willowbrook-bodied BMMO C3 coaches, is carefully reversed into the yard alongside Wellington garage in 1966 under the guidance of a man in a brown 'cow gown'. This coach was particularly associated with Leicester Southgate Street. There were 12 more coaches of very similar appearance, apart from extra glazing at roof level and fewer seats for extended-tours work, known as the C4 class. The first was bodied in 1953 by Carlyle and acted as design prototype for the remaining 11 C4s, bodied by Alexander, and the C3s, which all entered service in 1954. *Tennent's Trains, Halesowen*

Back Platform

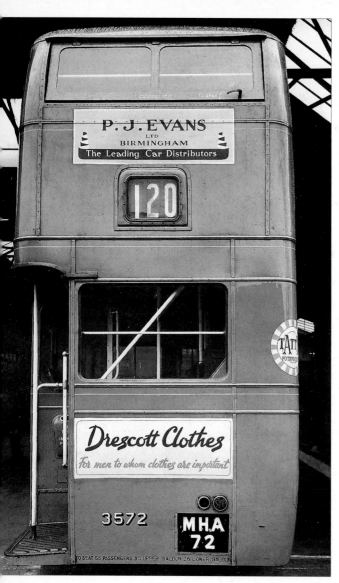

Above: Journey's end. GD6 class Guy Arab III 3572 runs back into garage. *C. J. Davis collection*

As the book draws to a close, you may be fancying something to settle your thirst. The tightly-packed itineraries of my friends and me in our school years took no account of the need for refreshment, and I guess it would have needed around a fortnight without food and sustenance before our bus-charged batteries began to run down. I don't recall us taking opportunities to refuel, apart from battling into the occasional Jubbly — for the youngsters, this was an orange drink, sometimes frozen, contained within an indescribable triangular package, almost impossible to open without spilling the contents when in its unfrozen form.

I hope the reminiscences have brought back a few memories to older readers, and offered a different approach to a great bus company to younger ones. The photographs have, of course, been the primary source of help here. I should like to thank the photographers for their ready assistance, especially those who fed and watered me during pleasurable all-day trawls through their collections, and also Mike Jordan of BaMMOT at Wythall and Mike Greenwood for their contributions to the search for illustrations. Paul Gray, as ever, made helpful contributions to the text, which also benefited from the reminiscences of many friends. Lots of information sources have bolstered the text, and I offer particular thanks to Ron Thomas. We should all be grateful for the work of the Omnibus Society and the PSV Circle, but especially to a wonderful man called Peter Hardy, sadly no longer with us, whose researches are at the root of any work on Midland Red. It was Peter, around 30 years ago, who suggested to the Publishers that a young man called Malcolm Keeley might make a decent job of a book they wanted written, and thus set me on my alternative career in transport writing. Thankyou, Peter.

Back cover: Ludlow garage's LD8-class Leylands were familiar in Shrewsbury on the X34/35. No 4063, however, was working out of Shrewsbury's own garage on a town service in July 1966. The LD8 was Leyland's endeavour to resemble Midland Red's D7, such as 4747 loading alongside. *Malcolm Keeley*

Front cover: The arrival of Digbeth's first D9s, 4849/53/5, was a source of great excitement for the author and his friends early in 1960, and the drivers looked pretty happy about it too. By June 1969, first production D9 4849 was just another bus when seen on the Stratford Road opposite Brandon Road in Hall Green, *en route* from central Birmingham early one morning prior to a better-patronised inbound peak journey. Most of the author's Midland Red days out began and ended on the company's Stratford Road services. *Malcolm Keeley*